This Book
Is Presented
To

_____

By

_____

On This Day

_____

Songs From The Heart

Compiled by
Mary Beckwith

Evergreen Communications, Inc.
Ventura, California

SONGS FROM THE HEART
A Practical Look at the Book of Psalms

Published by:
Evergreen Communications, Inc.
2085 Sperry Avenue
Ventura, CA 93003

© 1990 by Mary Beckwith. All rights reserved.
No portion of this publication may be reproduced in any form, except for brief quotations in reviews, without prior written permission of the publisher.

Scripture quotations in this publication are taken from:

AMP—From *The Amplified Bible.* Old Testament copyright © 1965, 1987 by The Zondervan Corporation. The Amplified New Testament copyright © 1958, 1987 by The Lockman Foundation. Used by permission.

KJV—*King James Version.*

NASB—Scripture taken from the *New American Standard Bible,* © 1960, 1962, 1963, 1968, 1971, 1972, 1973, 1975, 1977 by The Lockman Foundation. Used by permission.

NIV—From the *Holy Bible, New International Version.* Copyright © 1973, 1978, 1984 International Bible Society. Used by permission of Zondervan Bible Publishers.

NKJV—From the *New King James Version.* Copyright © 1979, 1980, 1982, Thomas Nelson Inc., Publishers. Used by permission.

RSV—From *Revised Standard Version* of the Bible, copyrighted 1946 and 1952 by the Division of Christian Education of the NCCC, U.S.A.

TEV—From the *Good News Bible*– Old Testament: Copyright © American Bible Society 1976; New Testament: Copyright © American Bible Society 1966, 1971, 1976.

TLB—Scripture verses are taken from *The Living Bible* © 1971 owned by assignment by Illinois Regional Bank N.A. (as trustee). Used by permission of Tyndale House Publishers, Inc., Wheaton, IL 60189. All rights reserved.

Library of Congress Cataloging-in-Publication Data

Songs from the heart / compiled by Mary Beckwith.
     p. cm. — (A Practical look at the book of Psalms; bk. 1)
     ISBN 0-926284-03-7 : 9.95
     1. Bible. O.T. Psalms—Meditations I. Beckwith, Mary A.,
     1945- . II. Series.
BS1430.4.S64 1990
242'.5—dc20   90-32491
                                              CIP

96 95 94 93 92 91 90 9 8 7 6 5 4 3 2 1
Printed in the United States of America

Songs From The Heart
is
Dedicated with love
to
Genevieve and Tanya,
Sisters in Christ

ACKNOWLEDGMENTS

We gratefully acknowledge the following authors and publishers for allowing us to excerpt from previous published works:

For the devotion entitled "Joy, Peace, Love, and Hope" by Fay Angus:
Excerpt from *Running Around in Spiritual Circles* by Fay Angus. Copyright © 1986 by Fay Angus. Reprinted by permission of Harper & Row, Publishers, Inc.

For the devotion entitled "Trusting God" by Catherine Marshall:
From the book *A Closer Walk* by Catherine Marshall, copyright 1986 by Calen Inc. Used by permission of Chosen Books Publishing Company, Ltd., Old Tappan, NJ.

For the devotion entitled "More Than the Sand?" by Eugenia Price:
Excerpt from *Another Day* by Eugenia Price, copyright © 1984 by Eugenia Price. Used by permission of Doubleday, a division of Bantam, Doubleday, Dell Publishing Group, Inc.

For the devotion entitled "H-E-A-V-E-N" by Corrie ten Boom:
From the book *Tramp for the Lord* by Corrie ten Boom with Jamie Buckingham, copyright 1974 by Corrie ten Boom and Jamie Buckingham. Used by permission of Fleming H. Revell Company.

In each case, the Scripture verses at the beginning of each devotion and the prayers at the end have been provided by the compiler.

Special thanks go to the writers across the country who have contributed to this work and to our prayer partners along the way.

May God bless those who have written and those who will read the messages contained in this book.

"Praise the Lord, for the Lord is good; sing to his name, for he is gracious!" (Psalm 135:3, *RSV*)

Welcome to **Songs From The Heart**

The Book of Psalms is the backdrop for this collection of devotions written from the hearts of over one-hundred and forty women from across the country.

We know that your own heart will be touched as you meet the writers in *Songs From The Heart.* Many of them are just like you, for they are women in tune to what it means to be a busy woman of the '90s; they are women in transition, as they change life roles and move about in our mobile society; and they are women in training, maturing to be all that God desires them to be.

The Psalmist sang out, "The Lord is my strength and my song," (118:14). As you're encouraged by the writings contained in *Songs From The Heart,* may you, too, see the Lord as your strength and your song.

The Publishers

CONTENTS

My Path in Life

Gloria Anderson

*Show me the path where I should go, O
Lord; point out the right road for me to
walk. Lead me; teach me; for you are the
God who gives me salvation.*
Psalm 25:4–5, *TLB*

World peace is something we strive
for but never quite achieve. And in this day when there is
so much turmoil all around us, it's not easy to find inner
peace.

After all, when we see Christian churches divided, we
wonder where peace can be found. Sometimes the
people we revere—like priests, TV evangelists, and
ministers—lose our respect; we wonder whom to trust.

When we fail to measure up to some task or to
others' expectations, we doubt our own abilities. When
our friends forsake us, we feel betrayed. When every
door seems to close before us, we cringe at life's
unfairness. We become hurt, disillusioned, and frustrated;
we struggle to find our way in an unfriendly world.
Discouraged, we each cry out, "Lord, save me...point out
the right road for me to take. Teach me the way of thy
salvation."

It's then that we realize inner peace can only be

found in knowing Jesus Christ. Jesus says, "I am the Way—yes, and the Truth and the Life." (John 14:6, *TLB*).

Yes, finding peace in a world of unrest seems next to impossible. But, when times are rough, it's comforting to recall Jesus' words before He ascended into heaven. He promised to send the Holy Spirit to teach us all things (John 14:26). And then He said, "I am leaving you with a gift—peace of mind and heart! And the peace I give isn't fragile like the peace the world gives. So don't be troubled or afraid" (verse 27).

Thank You, dear Lord, for sending Your Holy Spirit to teach and comfort us and to point out the path that leads heavenward. Thank You that in this world of unrest we can find the gift of peace of mind and heart in You. Amen.

Gloria Anderson has written numerous poems and articles. She enjoys crafts, sewing, hiking, traveling, research, and reading. Gloria and her husband, Charles, have four grown children and reside in East Wenatchee, Washington.

What a Difference an Hour Makes

Niki Anderson

*I wait for the Lord, my soul doth wait, and
in his word do I hope.* Psalm 130:5, *KJV*

When my husband installed a
stereo radio and cassette player in my car, I discovered a
bonus—a small digital clock. Through the months ahead,
I enjoyed the convenience of knowing the correct time
while I was driving. The day that daylight savings time
changed to standard time, I traded convenience for
confusion.

Because I misplaced the instructions for setting the
clock, I was stuck with a clock set one hour fast. Over
and over again, I would subtract one hour from the read-
out to determine the correct time. Months of this mental
computing became an annoyance.

In addition to my own frustration, others were
bothered. That clock aroused continual consternation

and comments. My daughter first noticed the time discrepancy. "Mom, I hope that clock is wrong. I can't be an hour late to cheerleading practice!"

Friends traveling with me would ask, "Niki, is that the correct time, or am I really mixed up today?"

When my second-grade son came home from school and told me he learned to tell time, I braced myself. Sure enough, during the next car ride, he remarked about my clock. "Mommy, do you know that clock is wrong?" he asked, as he compared the time on his new wristwatch.

I felt like screaming, but fumed silently. *Of course I know it's wrong. This is my car; I drive it nearly every day. Shouldn't I know? Besides, all the family and half my passengers have commented about my erring clock.*

Early in spring, I noticed a sign in a school yard. "April 4, Spring Ahead One Hour." *Happy day*, I thought. Soon this troublesome clock will be set right again. No more mental time adjustments to make, and no further comments from my passengers. What a relief it was the day everyone else moved their clocks ahead one hour, making my car time display accurate again.

My experience reminds me of the adage, "Time heals all things." The passing of time resolved my problem in a very literal manner.

Indeed, time seems to answer and end many difficulties in life. Like my clock, some trials goad us daily. They remind us of the seeming errors of life. Worst of all, such trials require us to do the hardest thing of all…wait. Wait until God accomplishes His purpose.

Then at last, we notice God's signpost announcing, "Trial Ended, Relief Ahead." How we rejoice.

What a difference an hour made in making me thankful for an accurate timepiece. What a difference a lengthy trial makes in shaping Christian character.

Dear Lord, give me the grace I need to endure the

spiritual time-tests that will develop in me the fruit of longsuffering. Amen.

Niki Anderson is the author of several articles. Besides writing, she enjoys teaching Bible studies and encouraging other women. She also teaches writing classes. Niki is married and the mother of two children. The Andersons enjoy cycling together and make their home in Spokane, Washington.

We Shall Go Rejoicing

Darlene Sybert Andree

This is the day which the Lord has made:
Let us rejoice and be glad in it.
                    Psalm 118:24, *NASB*

It wasn't a major undertaking; just load the furniture, books, and other belongings of my two sons into the family pickup and deliver them three hundred and fifty miles across the Cascade Mountains to their respective colleges in eastern Washington. One son would ride with me; the other would follow us in his 1975 Vega. The entire trip should only take seven or eight hours.

But the Lord saw what was ahead, as we could not, and gave us Psalm 118:24 that morning. We were reminded that God had made this day for us, and we were encouraged to adopt "rejoicing" as our attitude towards it.

The first hitch came after we were through the mountain pass and starting across the plains on the freeway. The Vega's engine died and resisted all efforts to revive it. But we were *glad* that the breakdown had occurred only a mile from a town where we could rent a tow bar.

Unfortunately, we parked too close to the light pole

in front of the rental shop and crumpled the mirror on the passenger side of the truck. As my son patiently removed the remnants, we were *glad* for the remaining mirror on the driver's side of the truck.

At the first son's college, we found his reserved room was locked and the key was lost; we were *glad* that a local locksmith was able to come to the rescue within thirty minutes.

With all the delays, it was two in the morning when the second son and I arrived at his college town. Of course, his dormitory was closed at that hour, but we were *glad* that the local motel was able to accommodate both of us, even though the reservation had been for one.

As we said good night, we realized that what might have been a day of dismay and frustration had been a day of adventure and laughter. It had created new bonds of respect and closeness between us, truly a gift from God.

Because we had remembered in the morning that God had made the day for us, we faced it with an attitude of anticipation. Instead of problems, we saw opportunities, as we searched for the solutions that we believed God had prepared in advance.

Lord, thank You for guiding our attitudes as well as our actions. Knowing You makes it realistic to rejoice in adverse circumstances. Help me to remember that every day is a gift from You and a time for gladness. Amen.

Darlene Sybert Andree has published numerous articles, devotions, and stories. She enjoys reading the classics and mysteries, canoeing, and cross-country skiing. Darlene has three sons. She makes her home in Cinebar, Washington.

Joy, Peace, Love, and Hope

Fay Angus

Happy is he whose...hope is in the Lord.
Psalm 146:5, *RSV*

The greatest hope for despair that the world has ever known came wrapped in swaddling clothes, lying in a manger.

In our home we keep the hope of Christmas visible and alive throughout the house the year around. We are a family that live and breathe tradition. We bake the heart-shaped cookies, color the eggs, carve the pumpkin, dress the turkey, and, most of all, we glory in the glory that is Christmastime.

From the time that they were born the children loved the wonder of the Christmas tree. Through the years we have developed a tradition of trimming the tree with handmade ornaments brought by little friends (the friends have now grown big, but they still want to make and bring their ornaments!). These are carefully packed away and pulled out again year after year as treasured tokens of friendships that we cherish and hope will last a lifetime through.

We each have our favorites. I have a smiling Grinch (making his topsy-turvy world right again, with hope renewed) painted by an artist friend. He goes on a middle branch, up front. The little angel in a crib, guarded by a mother and a father acorn bird, goes to the right and down low so children can both see and touch. We have high-up ornaments, low-down unbreakable ornaments, ornaments to be used as toys to be given to children who may come to visit [...].

Taking down the tree was always doom and gloom with tears of disappointment, so we thought up a new tradition. Each of us chooses a favorite ornament to hang about the house, anywhere we please, that we leave up the year around. These are the first off the tree and the first to be put back on. It reminds us that Christmas is never ever really past, and it keeps the hope of Christmas alive and visible daily in all our lives.

So if you come to visit us at any time at all, you will see hanging on the chandelier in the dining room, reflecting the brilliance of a thousand lights, a golden snowflake, twirling *joy* from a bit of thread.

On the door knob of the bathroom is a stuffed calico dove—*peace* purchased from a church bazaar. His wings are droopy now, so that he looks more like a seal with flippers flapping, and every time I take a bath I remind myself that I really must take a stitch here and there to perk him up, but then I never do!

Our daugthter chose a stained glass heart inscribed, "*Love* makes all things beautiful."

The ornaments we choose may change from year to year, but there is one that never changes. It hangs in the place of honor and has the greatest visibility—the entry hall—for everyone to see as they come in and out. It is a little wooden ornament carved around a child lying in a bed of straw. Above him is a shining star, its brightness is greater than the deepest darkness, and the light coming from that star fills our hearts with the presence of Christ always with us, he who is our *hope*.

Thank You, Father, for although our Lord came to us

wrapped in swaddling clothes nearly 2000 years ago, He is alive in my heart today! Amen.

Fay Angus, author and popular conference speaker, has written many books including *Between Your Status and Your Quo*, *Running Around in Spiritual Circles*, and *Heartstrings*. Because of her particular blend of faith and humor, she has been called "the evangelical Erma Bombeck." She and her husband make their home in Sierra Madre, California.

Meat in Due Season

Marlene Askland

The eyes of all wait upon thee; and thou givest them their meat in due season.
Psalm 145:15, *KJV*

After lifting the steaming skillet from the stove, I reached for the phone.

"Hi, Aunt Marlene, this is Brenda," came the friendly voice on the other end. "I have next week off, and I was wondering if it would be all right if I spend it with you folks."

"Sure," I told her. "When will you be coming?"

"The bus will arrive there at seven-thirty tomorrow evening," she replied.

My children were delighted that their cousin was coming for a visit, but I was a little apprehensive, for our cupboard was almost as bare as Old Mother Hubbard's.

"Lord, I don't know what I'm going to feed my family, to say nothing about an extra mouth," I complained.

The Lord reminded me of the time when our children were small and Grandma was visiting.

"What are we going to do for milk?" she asked. "These babies need milk!"

"The Lord will provide," we had assured her. "He does it all the time."

A few hours later, a woman knocked on the door and handed us two gallons of milk and a package of meat. Was Grandma surprised!

I felt ashamed for complaining now. A peace settled over me. I knew I could trust the Lord to provide. How He was going to do it was His business, not mine. My part was to keep my eyes fixed on Him.

The next evening my family and Brenda walked home after the Saturday night prayer meeting, but I had some things to do to get the church ready for Sunday morning, so I stayed behind.

When I went to my car to drive home, there was something in the back seat waiting for me. I praised the Lord all the way home. And when I arrived, I ran to the house shouting, "Come and see what the Lord did for us tonight!"

My husband, four children, and Brenda beat me back to the car. When they saw the seven packages of steaks, they, too, began to praise the Lord.

I had set my eyes on the Lord, and, once again, He gave us meat in due season.

Thank You, Lord, for not only giving us our daily bread, but for also giving us meat in due season. Help me never to take my eyes off You, my deliverer and provider. Amen.

Marlene Askland has published in previous devotionals and is currently studying with the Institute of Children's Literature. She enjoys calligraphy, decoupage, and painting. The Asklands have four grown children and make their home in Woodland, Washington.

Hidden Blessings

Marlene Bagnull

But as for me, I will sing each morning
about your power and mercy. For you have
been my high tower of refuge, a place of
safety in the day of my distress.
Psalm 59:16, *TLB*

"What am I supposed to do with those little boys? They won't get out of bed. They won't come and eat. They won't listen to anything I say."

"That's because they really aren't there, Mother," I used to try to assure her.

"What do you know?" she would snap. "I know what I'm talking about. I'm not blind or stupid. Last night they got into my dresser drawers again. You should see the mess they made. And they took my bar of soap and my comb. Why do they have to do stuff like that? Didn't their mother teach them any better?"

My mother has a dementing illness similar to Alzheimers. For the past two years, I have watched her lose more and more of her mind. Every day she sees people who aren't there and hears voices that aren't speaking.

Listening to her raving is the most difficult and painful thing I've ever experienced. "Why, God?" I've wept.

"Why can't You give her back her mind? Why are You allowing her to suffer like this?"

But, slowly, I've begun to see God's goodness, even in this. I've begun to see that my mother really isn't suffering. Because her mind is failing, she doesn't realize that she's getting worse. She doesn't always remember who I am, but she also doesn't remember people who have hurt her in the past. And even though she gets irritated with the "little boys" who are her daily companions, because of them she doesn't feel alone.

Day by day, oftentimes moment by moment, God is helping me to accept her as she is. He is helping me to listen to her and not argue with her. He is teaching me that I still can sing of His power and mercy. I feel His power undergirding me. And I know that in His mercy He will call my mother home when the time has come.

Help me, God, to see Your hidden blessings and to keep singing. Amen.

Marlene Bagnull is the author of two books and has published over 800 articles, stories, and poems. She is the director of the Greater Philadelphia Christian Writers Fellowship and teaches at several writers' conferences. Besides writing, she enjoys gardening and hiking. She and her husband, Paul, have three children and reside in Drexel Hill, Pennsylvania.

Watch Your Step

Lynn Baldemor

The Lord delights in the way of the man
whose steps he has made firm;...the Lord
upholds him with his hand.
Psalm 37:23, *NIV*

"We have a whole hour till dinnertime. Let's take a walk in the woods," my new friend, Nell, suggested that afternoon at our ladies' retreat.

I eagerly agreed. It was my first time at Silver Spur, and I had been dying to explore the place.

The trail led us to an almost dried-up creek. Some women from our camp were already there.

"Watch your step," someone called, as we approached. "Some of the rocks are slippery."

Nell was more surefooted than I, so I clung to her. Later, a little out of breath from the hike, my friend and I sat on the rocks with our feet dangling in the shallow water.

That incident reminds me of how often the Lord's strong hand has upheld me and my family in the last few years, making our steps firm. This was especially true regarding our coming to America from the Philippines.

Uprooting our family to live in another country was a

major step. It was not easy to leave friends, relatives, our jobs, a new house, and a lovable liver-spotted Dalmatian. After more than a year of seeking God's will, however, we felt convinced that He wanted us to move. Once sure, everything else fell into place, and the Lord provided for all our needs.

Our family of six got our visas without any problems. A caring brother-in-law looked after our dog. A nice family rented our home, and our travel expenses were met from savings, gifts, and the sale of most of our belongings. God even granted our request for a perfect time of departure—soon after the end of the school year for our children.

Once here, God met our needs, one by one.

Yes, there were trials along the way—"slippery spots." But true to His Word, God was there to guide our steps. He is a Father who delights in His children and He loves to guide them.

Father, thank You for upholding me with Your hand. Please direct my every step and make me obedient, no matter what lies ahead. Amen.

Lynn Baldemor has had numerous articles and poems published and has written evangelistic television specials for Philippine audiences. She enjoys crafts, swimming, cooking, and drama. She and her husband, Oscar, have four children and make their home in Long Beach, California.

Love Flowed

Victoria J. Bastedo

*Create in me a pure heart, O God, and
renew a steadfast spirit within me.*
Psalm 51:10, *NIV*

I remember the day I had wandered
so far away from God; I felt too weak to move. I couldn't
clean house; I could barely wash myself and the baby.
Finally, I couldn't hide from it anymore; bitter depression
set in. I tried to drag my withered spirit back to God, but
my voice was so parched from lack of His water, I could
hardly speak to Him.

"God!" I begged, "I'm so weak. Help me. Feed me.
Comfort me."

As the minutes wore on, my baby intruded on my
struggling. "Not now, Meribeth! Can't you see I'm too
weak to help you?"

She began to cry. It was almost her dinnertime, but I
didn't care. God wasn't helping me like I wanted Him to.
I grew desperate. But I couldn't give up; I needed Him!
Meribeth would just have to wait.

"When she stops crying," I said to myself, "I'll pick
her up."

She cried for fifteen minutes. Finally, in her misery,
she started to crawl away. And, finally, I realized my

hypocrisy. Here I had asked God to comfort and feed me, yet I had refused to comfort and feed my own child.

I picked Meribeth up and held her close, and love flowed. She became quiet now, but I began to cry—and repent.

As I fed my little girl her dinner, I began to feel strengthened. And the words written by King David in Psalm 51 were my food: "Create in me a pure heart, O God, and renew a steadfast spirit within me. Do not cast me from your presence or take your Holy Spirit from me. Restore to me the joy of your salvation and grant me a willing spirit, to sustain me."

O Lord, You do sustain me. Help me to be mindful today of the kind and loving parent I have in You. And in remembering, make me a loving parent to my child. Amen.

Victoria J. Bastedo attended Seattle Pacific University and has worked with young children for several years. She enjoys reading and building relationships with other people. She and her husband have one daughter. They make their home in Snoqualmie, Washington.

How Will God Save?

Kim Beaty

Now I know that the Lord saves his anointed; he answers him from his holy heaven with the saving power of his right hand. Psalm 20:6, *NIV*

"Oh, Dave," I gasped, horrified. "Look, there's another one, right on the counter." My husband took off his thong, crept across the kitchen with the stealth of a Zambesi warrior, and, then, wham! slammed the thong on a two-inch cockroach. "Oh, please," I begged, "take that disgusting thing out of here."

We were in rural Guatemala, moving into a house that had been closed up for months. Black, feeler-waving cockroaches had taken over the premises, fearlessly running across the floors and kitchen counters.

"Lord," I groaned, "I don't think I can handle this for five weeks."

The next day, Dave and I drove six hours back to the capital city. We stayed there a week, grocery shopping and rounding up supplies we would need. I prayed often during those seven days: "Lord, save me from those cockroaches when we go back. Either make them disappear or give me the courage to face them." I figured He'd pick the courage option.

When we returned to that country house, though, I didn't spot one cockroach in the kitchen. I put the groceries away, fixed supper, and then washed the dishes. Still no creepy bugs. Not even any telltale scurrying in the bowels of the cupboards. Had God actually banished them as I prayed? In the whole month that followed, I saw zero cockroaches in my kitchen.

I have not forgotten those five weeks. Sometimes the Lord puts me through situations so I learn to lean on His strength and sustaining power. But this time, He simply removed the things that caused my fear. He always knows just what kind of saving I need.

Father, thanks for caring about my fears. You reach down with Your hand and save me in the way You know is best. Amen.

Kim Beaty is on the editorial staff for Wycliffe Bible Translators and is working on her first book. She enjoys racquetball, cross-stitch, camping, and reading. Kim and her husband, Dave, make their home in Costa Mesa, California.

An Accident...
and God

Eileen M. Berger

*Hear my prayer, O Lord; let my cry for help
come to you.* Psalm 102:1, *NIV*

The wheels skidded and caught in
the snow piled beside the road. I went up over heaped
rocks and down the steep bank.

"Oh, Lord, help me," I cried. "There's nothing I can
do, but You can...."

The big car fell over onto its right side and rocked
there, but I couldn't tell what had prevented it from
landing on its roof in the middle of the creek.

*Dear God, please keep me calm. Help me to know
what's best for me to do.*

I considered climbing out the driver's window, but I
knew I must do nothing that might cause the vehicle to
roll over. On the other hand, there was the possibility
that the gas tank had ruptured when it scraped across the
piled stones. If so, there could be an explosion, so I
knew I'd better get out as soon as possible.

Please don't let me panic, Lord.

I cautiously released the seat belt and eased myself
down until I was standing on the passenger door, and
then kneeling there, I turned the window's handle. I took
the fact that the door was not dented too badly for the

window to roll down to be a sign that I should go out this way. The opening was about ten inches from the ice frozen at the water's edge—just enough for me to crawl through.

I didn't look back until I was out from under the car. When I did, I marveled that what had kept it from falling on me was a tree branch only two inches in diameter.

I had climbed back up the bank to the road before help arrived. X-rays showed no broken bones, and I went to work the next day, although weeks passed before I could move without back pain or discomfort.

What is most memorable about the whole experience, however, was my total awareness of God's presence, concern, and love. There was no fear, for He'd shown me once again that, "Lo, I am with you always"—even in an accident.

Dear Lord, help me to be always aware of Your presence and Your love. Amen.

Eileen M. Berger has written five books, and over one hundred stories, articles, and poems. She enjoys reading, researching, and being outdoors. Eileen is a medical technologist, married, and the mother of one daughter and two sons. The Bergers reside in Hughesville, Pennsylvania.

Cradled in God's Love

MarVel Dawn Berglund

*Yet Thou art He who didst bring me forth
from the womb; Thou didst make me trust
when upon my mother's breasts. Upon Thee
I was cast from birth; Thou hast been my
God from my mother's womb.*
Psalm 22:9-10, *NASB*

"I can't find a fetal heartbeat," proclaimed the doctor. "It's urgent we induce labor."

"But it's too soon," Mother exclaimed.

"We can't wait another hour, much less six weeks," was his curt reply. "Nurse..."

Later, in the hospital delivery room, Mother watched as the doctor held her preemie upside down and tenderly swatted its bluish-colored bottom. No cry. He tried again. Swoosh. The lungs were suctioned. The scrawny body of a baby girl hung limply from his sturdy hands. Another swat. Silence. "Nurse..."

"I'm sorry, Claire. We'll do all we can, but there is little chance for your daughter's survival. One lung is collapsed, causing her bluish coloring. She can't weigh over three pounds. It will take a miracle."

A prayer vigil began. Grandmas, grandpas, aunts, uncles, and friends were called upon to seek God's help on my behalf. They trusted God and He honored the meaning of my name, MarVel Dawn: miracle of the morning.

Cast upon Him from birth, He became my God. I think the very confidence placed upon God by that band of believers instilled faith and hope in my frail being, even when I was too weak to nurse. This heritage of faith has endured, sustaining me during difficult times of chronic illness directly related to my tenuous beginnings. When pain has reached intolerable levels, I have uttered despairing words like those of Job: "Why then hast Thou brought me out of the womb? Would that I had died and no eye had seen me!" (Job 10:18).

But God lovingly reminds me that His plan for my life is perfected in my obedience and trust in His purposes, even when I don't understand. To be handicapped in spirit is far worse than being crippled in body.

Lord, please forgive me when I fail to remember the miracle of life You gave to me. Instead of complaining about my pain, may I rejoice in this, a new day, to experience Your love and mercy. From You I receive strength to serve rather than to be served. Amen.

MarVel Dawn Berglund writes inspirationals, articles, and Bible studies. She enjoys sewing, crocheting, needlepoint, and lay counseling and has written, directed, and produced several drama presentations. MarVel and her husband, Bob, have three children and make their home in Poway, California.

Mom's Graduation Day

Delores Elaine Bius

But God will redeem my soul from the power of the grave: for he shall receive me. Selah. Psalm 49:15, *KJV*

When friends asked if I had prepared myself for the death of my mother, I reassured them that I had. However, it is one thing to intellectually accept a fact and quite another to deal with it emotionally.

Even though my mother was eighty-three and in poor health, it came as a shock when her doctor told her that tests showed she had cancer. Not only that, but she had pancreatic cancer, usually one of the fastest killing and most painful types.

Mom accepted the news with her usual equanimity. Her only question of her Christian doctor was, "How do the people cope who do not know the Lord?"

He replied, "They do not. They think this body, and this life, is the only one. They fall apart. But you and I have an invisible means of support, the Lord."

The next three months were heartbreaking for those of us who could only stand by and watch Mom growing weaker and weaker. She was soon confined to a wheelchair or bed, and her appetite disappeared.

Mom had always kept busy with all sorts of sewing

and crafts; she had read voraciously. Now, she no longer had the strength to do anything.

However, she still began each morning with her Bible reading and prayer and ended each day with prayer. In fact, as I cared for her during those months, she and I had wonderful times of prayer together each night.

The final two weeks of her life were spent in the hospital. Yet, miraculously, the intense pain the doctors had expected did not materialize. We could feel the many prayers ascending to heaven on her behalf being answered.

Even the last two days of her life, when she ceased to recognize any of us, she still knew her Lord. I overheard her praying out loud for the Lord to take her to heaven soon and to keep her loved ones from mourning for her too much.

God was gracious to allow me the privilege of being with my mother and holding her hand while He ushered her into His presence. How could I wish her back? That frail body of hers, so riddled with disease, and no longer functioning properly, was a prison for her at the end. Her soul escaped and went to be with the Lord: She graduated to heaven.

Oh, yes, I miss her dreadfully. But I sorrow not as those who have no hope, but with the assurance that I will see her again one day in heaven.

Father God, thank You that I can be assured that to be absent from the body means to be present with the Lord. The grave has no power over my loved one, for she is safe in Your presence! Amen.

Delores Elaine Bius has written over eight-hundred articles. She speaks for Christian Women's Clubs and retreats. Delores is a hospice worker and instructs at Christian Writers' Institute. She and her husband, Norman, have five grown sons and live in Chicago, Illinois.

The Laughing Box

Ami Blackshear

*Therefore my heart is glad, and my glory
rejoiceth: my flesh also shall rest in hope.*
Psalm 16:9, *KJV*

As a young girl, I remember
running into the living room of our friends' home, where
hanging on the wall was a colorful clown mask called a
laughing box. Underneath the grinning chin dangled a
fine, silver cord with a shiny, black ball on its end. When
the cord was lightly pulled, hilarious laughter echoed
throughout the house.

The cackles and chortles coming from the clown
were contagious. My entire family would join in with
gales of glee and silly giggles. Eventually we were all out
of control, bursting with belly roars. It was magical!

Today I live in a more complicated world. My
schedule has many pressures, with little time for play.
Some tasks seem so tedious. Others overwhelm me.
Daily encounters often shake the foundation of my
merriment and inner peace, cauterizing my heart with
scorching words or searing actions.

Sometimes I stand alone, rejected by a neighbor,
fellow worker, friend, or family member. My spirit is
broken. I'm caught off guard, at the brink of crumbling

inside. Then, glancing toward the coffee table, I see a fine, silver cord dangling from a shiny, black book. Pulling it gently breaks open the pages of my Holy Bible—the source of all happiness and security for me.

The Word of God is my laughing box. Jubilation echoes from its chapters. It is filled with a love that reaches beyond my feelings and perceptions to eternal truths. As I recall Christ's resurrection, my faith rises also. I dwell on hope, in anticipation of renewed dreams. It's a miracle!

I receive into my heart a heavenly laughter, triumphant hallelujahs ("In thy presence is fulness of joy) and the supernatural strength to just keep on rejoicing in "pleasures for evermore" (Psalm 16:11).

Precious Lord, thank You for the glorious blessings of gladness and restored hope, when I reach for Your Word and pull Your heart's cord. Amen.

Ami Blackshear is a commerical illustrator and has published a short story and numerous poems. She enjoys calligraphy, greeting card art, watercolor painting, and Japanese paper collage. Ami and her husband, Thomas, also an artist, work together out of their home in Novato, California.

A Shouting Sunset

Hilda J. Born

*And they who dwell in the ends of the earth
stand in awe of Thy signs; Thou dost make
the dawn and the sunset shout for joy.*
Psalm 65:8, *NASB*

It had been a long trip. Ten days
we'd been on the road before we finally reached my
brother's home. All I wanted was a few days to stay put.

Scarcely had we entered the house, when my sister-
in-law suggested we take two days to go to a rocky point
that juts into the Pacific Ocean. Trying to be a considerate
guest, I agreed to go along.

After an hour of city traffic, we got to the dusty
sideroads and drove through cactus country. Eventually,
we found the outcropping by the ocean and walked
down for a swim.

Before our eyes, the horizon changed. As the sun
came to rest at the end of the day, the whole firmament
was bathed in color. The vast stretches of water reached
up to the golden mantle of the setting sun. First, it was a
huge red ball and then it blended into radiant hues of
rose and purple.

Gazing at the splendor, we were awed and scarcely
spoke. Then the wonder of the colorful display excited

us to exclaim with praise and admiration, as we tried to capture a bit of it on film.

Bright stars came out when the purple became black velvet night. Soon we slept peacefully.

A wild bird's cry lured me out at dawn. Once again, the arrival of the sun was heralded in splendid hues. Although softer now, the pastels were just as overwhelming. Together with the gentle ocean breeze, this view had wiped away the exhaustion of the long road. I was filled with exhilaration and praise.

For all the beauty of the earth, the daily dawn and glorious set of sun, I shout Your praise, O Lord! Amen.

Hilda J. Born has written a variety of articles. She enjoys gardening, crewel embroidery, reading, traveling, and hosting friends and relatives. Hilda and her husband, Jacob, have five grown children and live in Matsqui, British Columbia.

No Backspace Key on the Tongue

Catharine Brandt

*O Lord, you have searched me and you
know me. Before a word is on my tongue
you know it completely, O Lord.*
Psalm 139:1,4, *NIV*

For years, I had trouble under-
standing those words in Psalm 139. How could God
know what I was going to say even before I spoke?

I knew that He is omniscient, all-knowing. But how
could He know my thoughts? What if I changed my mind?

Then, I began working with a personal computer,
and a light flashed on. Just as I had programmed the
computer and knew what was stored in its memory, so
God had, to a far greater degree, programmed me. He
knows all about me, because He created my inmost
being.

The big difference is that I'm only operating the
computer. I didn't fashion it. I have trouble
understanding how it works. But the Psalm tells me I am
fearfully and wonderfully made. As my Maker, the Lord
knows every word on my tongue. And unlike a
computer, I have free choice, which gets me into trouble
at times.

Many times, when the computer fails to obey my

commands, I am ready to give up. I'm glad the Lord never gives up on me. I don't like to think of the times I've been unworthy of His trust and have failed to produce what He expects of me. I need to pray about that unruly member, my tongue, and ask God to program my thoughts so that my words will please Him.

The Apostle James tells us the tongue gets plenty of exercise, such as boasting, lying, gossiping, bossing, speaking unkind words, or speaking non-stop. Most of us have said words or expressed opinions we bitterly regret. But unlike a computer, there's no backspace key on the tongue. What's said cannot be deleted. The only remedy consists of repentence, forgiveness, and apology.

Lord, please take charge of my thoughts and words. Delete the ones You disapprove of, before I speak. Amen.

Catharine Brandt has written eleven books and over seven hundred articles. She is a volunteer at a nursing home and enjoys her collection of handbells. Catharine has one son and one daughter and resides in Minneapolis, Minnesota.

Message on a Garden Bench

Mary J. Brown

*We wait in hope for the Lord; he is our help
and our shield. In him our hearts rejoice,
for we trust in his holy name.*
Psalm 33:20-21, *NIV*

I smiled as I watched a baby baboon
scamper to his mother. She scooped him up under her
stomach where he clung as she ambled down the hill.
My husband, Alex, and I were in South Africa, where he
was conducting physics research and I was becoming
preoccupied with having a baby. We had been "trying to
get pregnant" for several months. Now, even watching
the antics of baby animals triggered my yearning for a
child.

On a hot, bumpy trip across the country, we stopped
at a town called Matjiesfontein, which our host described
as magical. During the long drive across dusty roads, my
mind had lingered in its usual place—wanting to be
pregnant—but Matjiesfontein lured me back to the
present. It was a lush island of green, in the midst of the
barren karoo of central South Africa.

We had a sumptuous dinner at the elegant Victorian
hotel. The next morning, before continuing our journey,
we walked through the gardens where verses of poetry

were inscribed on benches. After reading the message on one bench, I quickly rummaged through my purse for paper and pen. On the back of a receipt, I scrawled: "Live in the present. Be grateful for the past. Leave the future in God's hands."

That week I was better able to keep my thoughts in the here-and-now, where much was waiting to be enjoyed: a drive through a canyon of golden rock, ostriches peeking through fences, richly forested hills along the Indian Ocean.

When we returned home, we continued trying to start a family. One day, I discovered that paper in my purse. Every day after that, I renewed my commitment to savor the present and surrender my desires to God.

Eighteen months later, I became pregnant and now we have a daughter, Elizabeth. But those months of practice, of focusing on the here-and-now, help me as I confront the challenges of parenting or when anxieties about the future creep into my thoughts. In fact, I keep that slip of paper handy and pray often:

Lord, help me to enjoy Your blessings in the present, to be thankful for those in the past, and to leave the future in Your hands. Amen.

Mary J. Brown has published in numerous Christian magazines. She has traveled to several countries and enjoys teaching Sunday School and piano, gardening, and family bike trips. She and her husband, Alex, have one daughter and reside in East Lansing, Michigan.

The Perfect Gift

Margaret Brownley

Be still, and know that I am God.
Psalm 46:10, *KJV*

Recently, I came across a diary written by a young girl nearly a century ago. She had written how she'd been blessed by the Lord with myopic eyes. She went on to say that when the snow fell, her blurred vision turned the world into a beautiful "lace" wonderland.

Since I've had to wear glasses all my life, this was an eye-opener. Never had I considered poor vision a divine gift. My imagination stimulated, I went a whole day without my glasses, and it was like living in a magic kaleidoscope of changing shapes and colors. The world seemed softer, less harsh. A young girl had reached across time to give me a perfect gift.

I used to spend hours searching for the perfect gift for each person on my Christmas list. But that was before I understood that such gifts can't always be bought. Most perfect gifts come from within, during an exquisite moment when the receiver and the giver are in true accord.

I received one such gift from a friend who called to read me a poem she'd written. Imagine my delight upon learning that it had been something I had inadvertently said to her that had inspired the poem. My friend insisted I had given her a gift and was surprised when I told her that it was she who had given to me.

That's how it is with perfect gifts. The receiver and the giver become one. The perfect gift knows no boundaries, and we're never quite certain how or when one will appear.

What is the best way to prepare ourselves for both the receiving and the giving of perfect gifts? By keeping still and allowing room for gifts to transpire. I discovered that gem of a diary while sitting quietly in a library. The poem came out of a long leisurely lunch with a friend. The day I understood what it meant to be a Christian, and the full extent of God's gifts, I was at a retreat.

By spending leisurely time with friends and family, we allow for the possibility of both giving and receiving the perfect gift.

God, help me to remember that only by receiving fully and giving freely can I become one with You, for You are the giver of perfect gifts. Amen.

Margaret Brownley has written and published six books and numerous articles. In addition, she writes two monthly columns and teaches novel and fiction writing. Margaret and her husband, George, have three grown children and make their home in Simi Valley, California.

One Mother's Song

Cynthia I. Buckingham

The Lord is my strength and my shield; My heart trusts in Him, and I am helped; therefore my heart exults, and with my song I shall thank Him. Psalm 28:7, *NASB*

Single parent. I never would have guessed what an impact being a mother would have on me. Even though the joys far outweigh the sorrows, there's the constant worry of nurturing and providing. But the Lord takes on a special role with us single moms. For just as we provide for our children, He provides for us.

It was, of course, through a child's eyes that I watched my own single mother raise two girls alone. Even though we had the things we needed, my mother struggled hard to provide them, often at the cost of not being home with us. I am finding out that I did not understand my mother's role then.

Over the last few years, I've been faced with my own stirring feelings, from the most uplifting, the birth of my baby girl, to the lowest, a sudden divorce. I came to realize I had deep fears within myself. So, my walk to discovery began as I sought help through counseling and friends.

I found out that saying "I'm a Christian" wasn't

57

enough; I needed to claim my commitment daily. I was reminded there are choices I can make: God has given me the freedom to decide whether or not I will follow Him. And when I do, I receive the guidance and confidence I need to face life, and most importantly to receive His love.

With God's help, I have come to understand how my childhood affected my adulthood. Each generation may be different in appearance, but they all pass down some of the same characteristics—from embracing love to dying hurts. My deepest desire is now for the freedom to end negative habit patterns and develop positive, godly ones. This, as a single mother, is my prayer for my daughter...and for myself!

Understanding my fears, alone, does not solve the problems, but it does give me peace. And every day I feel God's beloved assurance, assurance that He will cause me to succeed at my most treasured profession—motherhood.

My soul cries out for the needs I have as a parent. But, Lord, You fill each day with Your grace so my heart can be peacefully secure. Amen.

Cynthia I. Buckingham, besides writing, enjoys sewing, homemaking, skiing, biking, and being a mother. She is a preschool teacher's assistant and recently ended a seven-year position as county extension food advisor. Cynthia has one daughter, Cristina, and lives in Redmond, Washington.

My Miracle

Ellie Busha

*In my distress I called upon the Lord; to my
God I cried for help.* Psalm 18:6, *RSV*

It was a hot and humid summer day.
Our tiny, upstairs apartment was stifling. With much
effort I was able to raise a large window in the bedroom,
placing a stick to hold it up. None of the windows in the
apartment of the old Victorian-style home would remain
open without support.

I was busily cleaning the bedroom, when, suddenly, I
heard a bang and then a blood-curdling scream from my
two-year-old son. Though he was but a few feet from
me, I hadn't seen him toddle to the window and
somehow knock the support from its place. The window
had fallen shut, jamming little Ricky's fingers between it
and the sill.

My heart raced wildly as I ran to the window to free
my precious son. In vain, I tried to lift the window; it
wouldn't budge. Harder and harder I struggled, but to no
avail. The window would not move.

I began to cry for help. No one answered. I called out
the name of the young boy who lived below. He didn't
hear.

Reaching a point of near-panic, with little Ricky still

screaming beside me, I cried, "Please, God, help me!" My hands remained on the window pulls, but I had no strength. I was helpless.

Suddenly, as though strong hands had been placed over mine, the window effortlessly floated upward.

Then, with one swift movement, I pulled my son to me. "Thank You, Lord," I cried over and over, as I tended to Ricky. Not one of his little fingers was broken or even bruised. How fully God had answered my cry for help!

Only those who understand the power of our great, prayer-answering God believe me when I testify that God performed a miracle for me that day.

Thank You, Father, for always being there when I need You. Thank You for being a prayer-answering and miracle-working God. Amen.

Ellie Busha has written devotions, poetry, and music. In addition, she has written and conducted Bible studies and workshops for women and teaches piano and organ. Ellie and her husband, Don, have six grown children and make their home in Fenton, Michigan.

No More!

Sue Cameron

*How lovely is your dwelling place, O Lord
Almighty! My soul yearns, even faints for the
courts of the Lord; my heart and my flesh
cry out for the living God.* Psalm 84:1-2, *NIV*

At breakfast Sunday morning the
children asked the familiar questions:

"Which church are we going to today?"

"Can we go back where they have goldfish crackers
at snack time?"

"Do we have to go to another church? I'm tired of
going to different churches!"

My husband looked at me from across the table; his
eyes said, "I'm tired, too."

I nodded my agreement and said, "Listen, kids, I've
heard the church we're trying this morning is a good
one. Who knows? It might be just the place for us."

I remember the confidence my husband and I felt
when we moved across the country. "It won't be easy to
leave family and friends," we told each other, "but as
soon as we find a church home we'll be fine." But we'd
been searching for over a year now.

I felt so isolated, like an uprooted flower in desperate
need of a place to be planted. I thought if we didn't find

61

a church soon, I'd shrivel up spiritually.

But God planted us that Sunday morning. When we first walked into that church, we knew we belonged there. We felt like we had come home at last!

During the worship service my parched soul began to revive. As I joined those around me in singing songs of praise, I responded with spontaneous tears of gratitude. At the preaching of the Word, something inside me stirred and began to grow again.

I wanted to stand up and shout, "It's so good to be here worshiping the Lord with all of you!"

In that moment, I determined to cherish the privilege of gathering for worship. There were times in my past when thoughts of "Oh, no, I've got to get the kids dressed and ready for church," would fill my mind. No more!

No more going to church out of a sense of duty or with drudgery. Now I understand how wonderful it is to be in the Lord's house, among His people. But I didn't treasure this experience until I lived without it for a season.

Lord, thank You for giving us the privilege of worshiping with other believers. Help me never to take it for granted. Amen.

Sue Cameron is the assistant director for the Greater Philadelphia Christian Writers Conference. She has authored articles and received awards for her poetry and enjoys drama, sacred dance, and crafts. She and her husband, Craig, have four children and reside in Morton, Pennsylvania.

Seers and Fortunetellers

Suzanne P. Campbell

*I will walk with integrity of heart within my
house; I will not set before my eyes anything
that is base.* Psalm 101:2–3, *RSV*

It was on a Wednesday night about
ten years ago that I learned God's agenda always takes
precedence. I've never forgotten and I try to apply that
lesson daily.

"Samuel was a prophet; a prophet is a kind of seer or
fortuneteller," I read, while preparing to teach the eighth-
grade confirmation lesson.

I was angry. "If Christian material compares God's
prophets to the fortunetellers or seers the kids see at
carnivals, no wonder they are so vulnerable to the
counterfeit messages they get from cults," I raged
inwardly. When I stopped to pray for guidance, an inner
voice prompted, "Don't teach this lesson; teach one on
the occult and tell the class why."

Wednesday night arrived and I faced the twelve
fourteen-year-olds with a certain trepidation. Many
attended these classes only to please their parents. Would
they even hear me? I sent up a quick prayer for wisdom
and began, "Kids, we are not going to do the lesson you

prepared for today, because God has made it clear there is something else He wants you to learn."

We opened our Bibles to Leviticus 19:31, "Do not turn to mediums or wizards; do not seek them out, to be defiled by them." We read in the last chapter of Revelation about the new Jerusalem, which will be entered by the righteous. "Outside are the dogs and sorcerers and fornicators and murderers and idolaters, and everyone who loves and practices falsehood."

The teens participated as never before and began to see parallels in their own lives. "We've been fooling around with Ouija boards at parties lately," said one young girl from a strong Christian family. "None of us realized that calling on spirits to predict the future was wrong. Maybe that's why God wanted you to teach this lesson."

The girl sitting next to her shook her head in wonder, "Do you mean that God really cares what we do, even when we're at parties?"

The class was never the same again; our discussions were lively and the kids were excited to know more about this God who loved and cared for them.

Heavenly Father, thank You for showing me that You care about every area of my life and that You're willing to give me direction, if I will only ask. Amen.

Suzanne P. Campbell has written many articles for magazines and newspapers. She teaches writing classes for all ages and is currently president of the Minnesota Christian Writers Guild. Suzanne enjoys traveling and hosting guests from other countries. She and her husband, Dick, have two children and make their home in Minneapolis, Minnesota.

A New Heart

Jan Carpenter

*Would not God find this out? For He knows
the secrets of the heart.* Psalm 44:21, *NASB*

I hated nursing homes! My mother
endured her last six years in one, and it was awful. I had
felt more helpless with each visit. Worst of all, it was a
reminder of my own vulnerability.

Yet, there I was, winding my way to a nursing home,
where our church sponsored weekly bingo games. I had
been able to escape going, until a friend asked me to fill
in for her. So that I wouldn't have to go alone, I talked
my two teenage daughters into joining me.

Arriving at the home, I nervously plodded down the
stairs, trailing behind my girls. Once in the room, that
helpless feeling swept over me again. The workers, on
the other hand, appeared capable, and my daughters,
chatting and smiling with the residents, acted like they'd
been doing this forever.

"Why am I here? They don't need me," I scolded
myself.

"Would you like to call the numbers today?" the director questioned.

"Sure," I answered, scared to death, but glad to feel needed.

Although the afternoon was going surprisingly well, I decided I would not return. Never again did I want to see this much pain at one time. There were people who couldn't see, people who couldn't hear, and one whose head was locked to her chest. One man was strapped to his chair so he wouldn't fall off; he had no legs to support him.

When the game was over, I fled home, anxious to shut out the horrible pictures. I prayed, "God, help those poor people."

As the weeks passed, something strange took place. I found myself with a peculiar yearning to go back to the nursing home. Giving in, I made my way down the short flight of stairs once again and walked into the bingo room.

Can this be the same place? I asked myself. *Look at all the smiling faces. Don't they realize this is a nursing home?*

Just then one of the residents waved. "Hi, Jan," she grinned. "I hope you'll call today. You have a nice voice."

It's been eleven difficult, but fulfilling, years since I first visited the home. Much has happened during those years: Florence, who liked my voice so well, attends church with me; regularly, I visit the bedridden residents; and, last fall, I began leading devotions there.

Yes, there is sadness, as well as good-byes to dear friends, but I shall be forever grateful for the new heart God has given me for the elderly in nursing homes.

There's no place I feel more needed and appreciated!

Thank You, Lord, for turning my fearful heart into a more loving heart. Help me to keep growing in You. Amen.

Jan Carpenter has written several devotions for other publications, as well as her own devotional book. Besides nursing homes, she visits a women's prison. She enjoys cooking, home decorating, and music. The Carpenters have two grown children and reside in Orono, Minnesota.

Letting Go

Lynn Casale

In my anguish I cried to the Lord, and
he answered by setting me free.
Psalm 118:5, *NIV*

I knelt at the gravestone and forced myself to look at the inscription. Seeing her name would make her death real, I knew.

Nineteen years had passed since the car accident that ended my best friend's life and nearly my own. I had appeared to accept the tragedy and continue with life, yet, subconsciously, for all those years, I had felt hurt and betrayed by God. My unexpressed rage had solidified into a distrustful, wounded mass.

I fingered a ring on the gravestone and discovered that it pulled up to form a vase. I filled it with water from a nearby faucet for the armful of daisies I had brought.

Daisies were her favorite. As I slowly stripped the bottom leaves from each stem and placed it in the vase, I reflected on the recent events that had brought me here. Gently, the Lord had exposed my hidden wound and lanced it, mercifully releasing my long-denied cries of abandonment and anger. "How could You have done this to me, knowing how deeply it would hurt? I feel so alone, so betrayed!"

My confession cleared the way for the warmth of God's healing love to melt my frozen rage. Finally, I was open to receive the comfort God had longed to give, taste His grace unaltered by my anger, and view the tragedy from a higher perspective. My pilgrimage to the cemetery commemorated this divine surgery.

I focused on the inscription again, allowing my memories to surface. I spoke aloud. "You were a wonderful friend. It was so hard to let you go. I pretended you never lived so I wouldn't have to acknowledge that you died. I'm sorry I did that to you." Tears long held in check flowed freely now. "You did live and you loved me well and I loved you too."

Amazingly, as I accepted her death, my clouded memories of her became vivid and clear. I could hear her hearty laugh, see her smiling eyes, feel the encouragement of her loving acceptance. The expression of my grief allowed me to embrace her memory, to treasure the joy of having been loved by a friend.

Feeling peaceful and whole, I wrapped the discarded leaves in the green florist paper. I spoke her name and said good-bye. I knew that at long last I had let her go.

I knew the Lord had set me free.

Lord, reveal those places in me that are in need of Your healing touch. Remove the obstacles in me that prevent the flow of Your love and grace. Hear my anguished cries and set me free. Amen.

Lynn Casale, besides writing, enjoys reading, journaling, cooking, sewing for her girls, helping at school, and gardening. In addition, she ministers to other women who were abused as children. Lynn and her husband, Jeff, have two daughters and reside in Oakland, California.

Striving or Peace

Shawn Lee Clark

Cease striving and know that I am God.
Psalm 46:10, *NASB*

Raising kids is no picnic! Sometimes the bickering and fighting are enough to put you right over the edge. And then they try pulling you into the battle; before you know it, you've started yelling and acting in ways you'd rather not.

One day, the girls got into a fight first thing in the morning. I had been up all night with the new baby, so after getting my husband off to work, I went back to bed instead of having my regular quiet time with the Lord. That was a mistake!

As I rolled out of bed, I found myself yelling and chasing the girls off to their rooms for time-out. It didn't take long for me to figure out that it would have been better for me to sacrifice my sleep rather than go without meeting the Lord in the morning.

As I am writing this, I realize this fighting between the girls is a mirror of the same struggle I see within myself—my flesh versus the Spirit. It's when I choose to surrender my fleshly desires and old behaviors that the process of "dying to self" can take place, and the striving and fighting become less and less. As I give up having it "my way," I find God's peace settling within me, which allows the Holy Spirit to fill me with the fruits of love, joy, peace, patience, kindness, goodness, faithfulness, gentleness, and self-control (Galatians 5:22-23)—all important things you need to have when raising kids!

Dearest Heavenly Father, help me to surrender all to You and allow the Holy Spirit to fill me anew. Amen.

Shawn Lee Clark, besides writing, enjoys running, soccer, reading, loving friends, and praying. She and her husband, Timothy, have two daughters and one son and reside in Duvall, Washington.

Refuse to Be Intimidated

Joan Clayton

The Lord is the stronghold of my life—of whom shall I be afraid? Psalm 27:1, *NIV*

We didn't realize the potential growth of our trees when we set them out as seedlings. With the passing of time, the trees grew, branched out, and began touching each other. We noticed that the strongest trees would intimidate the weaker ones. The weaker trees would lean as far away as possible from the prevailing trees. That is, all but one! The evergreen refused to be intimidated.

Through the years, the evergreen has grown straight up, pushing through the confining branches of the nearby locust tree. Although not very wide, the evergreen is tall and stately.

Daily, you and I are surrounded by situations that would threaten to unnerve us. And, like the weaker trees, we can lean away in fear, or, like the evergreen, we can boldly stand tall and refuse to be intimidated.

Knowing that an all-wise and loving, heavenly Father is with me, I can take courage and boldly declare: "The Lord is the stronghold of my life—of whom shall I be afraid?"

Are you facing a difficulty today? Take courage. Rise

up and grow strong and tall in the midst of your surroundings. If a tree can do it, so can you and I!

Precious Lord, I thank You and praise You. In You, I have all the strength I need to stand tall. Amen.

Joan Clayton is a book author and has had articles appearing in numerous publications. Besides writing, she enjoys oil painting, piano, gardening, and country crafts. She is married and the mother of three grown sons. The Claytons reside in Portales, New Mexico.

Seven Times Do I?

Paula Cook

*Seven times a day do I praise thee
because of thy righteous judgments.*
Psalm 119:164, *KJV*

When I start each day with praise to the Lord, I start the day without woes. When I awake with praise on my lips and in my heart, the day is brighter.

But praise doesn't stop in the morning; it continues throughout the day, for with praise, the dark clouds of "poor me" disappear, and the *Son*shine breaks through.

And then, I praise the Lord at mealtime, for He has supplied and given, as He has promised, the sustenance and strength I will need for the day.

I praise the Lord when things go wrong as well as right. I praise Him at the time of a task, and the task is easier and lighter. I praise the Lord when my boss says, "Work late tonight."

I praise the Lord when the children are troublesome, for the Lord gave them as a blessing. I praise the Lord while I do housework, for He is there and worthy of my praise.

I praise the Lord before going to sleep, for He has been with me during the day. I praise the Lord for answers to prayer; He never fails. I praise the Lord for all the things He has done and will do. I praise Him forevermore.

Yes, He is worthy of my praise.

Lord, I give You all my praise, for without You I am and have nothing. Lord, You are my Savior, my Healer, and my life. Thank You, Lord, for hearing all my prayers. Amen.

Paula Cook, besides writing, enjoys "meeting people and talking to the Lord." In addition, she teaches Bible classes and speaks to church groups. Paula and her husband, Bill, have three grown sons and make their home in Corinth, Mississippi.

Work Out!

Patti Townley Covert

*Establish my footsteps in Thy word, And do
not let any iniquity have dominion over me.*
Psalm 119:133, *NASB*

Jazzercise—I'll do it! Aerobics with a
beat. Music pulsating from inside of me out, into a dance
that will tighten my muscles and strengthen my heart.

Sluggish and weary from too much inactivity, I'm
determined to get in shape. Physically, it has become
hard to meet life's demands and I need my body to last.
Discipline will develop habits of exercise. I'll have to
work out, especially when I don't feel like it.

Loud music, fans whirring, sweat dripping—women
tuning their bodies to the beat. Watching someone in
front of me, I start moving in step. Oh, oh, she's got it
wrong! It's safer to keep my eye on the teacher, who
really knows the routine. Whirl, sway, slide, kick. Out of
sync, my feet don't want to move the right way.

The steps come easier with practice and the rhythm
becomes more natural. I relax and smile, throwing
myself into each movement, pushing to the limit.

1, 2, 3...5, 6, oops! This is new. Count, watch, pay
attention. Sore muscles all over again. But I'm learning
the only way to get rid of flabby places is by working

past the pain. And stretching out those muscles afterwards feels so good.

It's even more important for me to be determined to work out in God's gym, as my spiritual body will last forever. I need to go where my steps will become established in His ways. Looking to my Instructor, I learn how to work past the pain life brings—expecting and accepting it, allowing Him to use it to make me strong.

Excess weight of sin and poor choices begins to come off as I work at tightening muscles of obedience. Sometimes it's hard to get my feet to go the right way and I end up sore. But when I set myself to line up with Him, I'm being stretched spiritually and that feels good. As I pick up the steps, His music is beginning to play out in my life.

Father God, please teach me the steps of living life Your way. Strengthen me by Your Word and enable me to be obedient. Amen.

Patti Townley Covert enjoys reading, gardening, Jazzercize, playing Frisbee and Smashball, going to the beach and Bible study. In addition, she operates a typing service from her home. Patti and her husband, Tim, have two sons and make their home in Ontario, California.

The Soggy Cat

Michelle J. Cresse

The sacrifices of God are a broken spirit; a broken and contrite heart, O God, you will not despise. Psalm 51:17, *NIV*

My three-year-old son rustled through his dresser. My gym bag lay at his feet and he was stuffing clothes into it. He reached for socks, and I asked, "Gordon, what are you doing?"

"Running away." He wouldn't look at me.

"Oh," I said and went back to the living room.

Gordon came out of his room with the long strap of the gym bag over his shoulder; the bag dragged across the floor behind him. Solemnly, he walked past me to the door and stopped.

When he didn't move, I asked, "Gordon, are you mad because Mommy punished you?"

He nodded.

"Do you know why you were punished?" I asked.

"Because I put the cat in the toilet?"

"Haven't I told you not to put the cat into the toilet?" Another nod. "But you did it anyway."

I put out my hand and Gordon took it.

"I love you, Gordon. It would hurt me terribly if you ran away. But Mommy and Daddy have rules. If you can't obey the rules, maybe you don't want to live here."

Gordon's arms wrapped around my neck. "I'm sorry, Mommy! I won't wash the cat anymore."

Later, I reflected on the day with a slight sense of amazement. My son, as he dipped the cat, knew he would be in trouble. That's why he jumped three feet when I caught him. Yet, *he* was angry with me!

How easy it is to project blame. I know where Gordon acquired this trait. He got it from me. When I sin, I hate to admit it. It's easier to blame circumstances, daily pressures—even God. Faced with the consequences of my actions, I want to run away. The child inside sticks her lower lip out and says, "God doesn't love me."

But if I acknowledge my sin, God wraps me in His forgiving embrace. His heart is tender toward a contrite spirit. Reconciliation with God is always an "I'm sorry" away.

The cat and I forgave Gordon. We had a wonderful reunion.

Dear Lord, help me to accept responsibility for my sins and to come to You when I feel like running away. Amen.

Michelle J. Cresse has published several articles and two books. Her interests include skiing, softball, public speaking, reading, and working with her husband with the teens at her church. The Cresses have three children and reside in Roy, Washington.

Tomato Juice and God

Janet Crotty

Wash away all my iniquity and cleanse me from my sin. Psalm 51:2, *NIV*

The smell made its way quickly down the hall and into the bedroom. Whomp! It hit my nostrils like a slap across my face and I knew immediately what had happened.

"Oh, no!" I heard my husband cry loudly from the kitchen. I ran down the hall to find our lovable Scottie dog rolling around in her bed trying to escape the horrible odor that had now invaded the entire house. "The skunk made a bull's-eye," my husband groaned.

"What do we do now?" chimed in one of our boys. "Throw her outside to live? We can't keep her in the house. That smell makes me want to throw up!"

"No!" protested the other son. "Annie is used to being inside with us. We can't just throw her away!"

"Quick," I ordered, "go to the neighbors and get me as many cans of tomato juice as you can. I've heard it washes away the skunk odor and makes the dog smell as good as new."

I picked up Annie and carried her at arm's length down the hall to the bathtub. We were both having a difficult time trying to cope with the horrible smell.

"Here are two large cans of tomato juice!" cried one son. In the meantime, our pitiful dog was trying to hide at one end of the bathtub. I began to pour the tomato juice over Annie. My two sons stood over me, both equipped with noseplugs.

"How can you stand to wash her, Mom? She smells awful!"

As the red juice covered Annie thoroughly, the analogy became clear. "I'm washing Annie because I love her. I want her to be able to live in our house and sit in my lap. If I did not wash her, we would have to keep her outside the house at a distance, and she would no longer be our pet.

"Did you know, boys, that's why God sent Jesus to die for us? God loves us so much, but our sins smell as bad as skunk odor to God and He can't get near to us. He so wants to have us live with Him in heaven and to cuddle us in His lap, even while we are still here on earth. But we cannot approach Him as long as we smell terrible like a skunk.

"Just like the tomato juice is cleaning up Annie and taking away that awful smell, so Jesus' blood is the only thing that can wash away our sins so we can come near to God."

As the juice washed the last of the skunk odor down the drain, making our lovable dog lovable again, we could rejoice that the blood of Jesus Christ continually washes away our sins as we come to Him. Then we can come boldly into our heavenly Father's presence.

Dear Heavenly Father, I know there are still areas in my life that are unpleasing to You and smell as bad as any skunk. Help me to continually submit myself to the precious cleansing blood of Jesus so that I can remain in close fellowship with You. Amen.

Janet Crotty has written Sunday School curriculum, puppet shows, and a Bible study. She enjoys hiking, boogy boarding at the beach, reading, and working with teens in their Christian development. She and her husband, Dan, have two sons and reside in Ventura, California.

Sow in Tears; Reap in Joy

Kay David

*Those who wept as they went out carrying
the seed will come back singing for joy.*
Psalm 126:6, *TEV*

For years, my reaction to painful, emotional darts led to defeat and wastefulness. After a hurt, I would run home, find a blanket, and sleep. This would be followed by a search for delicious food, a time of dozing, and then a "pity party."

But I learned that God's plan for responding to suffering is different. Shortly after a recent, hurtful event, I left for church, alone. Driving down the highway, my tears erupted. "Lord," I cried, "I'm not able to teach today."

"I will help," flashed through my mind.

The tears stopped as I entered the church parking lot. Wiping my face and grabbing my supplies, I headed off to sow the seeds of God's love in the lives of the children.

After class, a parent informed me that her daughter loves class. "You have a natural flair for working with children," she said.

"Thank you," I replied. "God is the natural."

God says, "Go sow, even in brokenness, and I will help.

Lord, help me not to return to my old ways of reacting to suffering. Help me to sow goodness even while I am suffering. Amen.

Kay David has written for the *Upper Room* and *Pathways to God.* She enjoys reading, being a retreat speaker, and teaching. Her family lives in the country and raises llamas. Kay and her husband have two children. They reside in Greenacres, Washington.

Worrying Foolishly

Kimberly De Jong

*Those who know your name will trust in
you, for you, Lord, have never forsaken
those who seek you.* Psalm 9:10, *NIV*

A few days before our recent
camping trip, I began to worry about money. I worried
until I felt physically ill. I knew it was foolish to worry.
Worrying hadn't changed situations in my past; it
wouldn't now. I had to remind myself that God always
takes care of my needs.

Since my husband and I bought our own business six
years ago, I have begun to worry when payments stop
coming in the mail. At times, when customers don't pay
their bills, our own begin to pile up. Every month or so,
we face these "dry spells." And I begin to worry.

It's so easy to forget that God is watching over me.
He knows my every need and will provide a solution. I
know I need to put my trust in Him, but sometimes I
forget the times I've faced in the past and how God
provided for my needs then. The bills were paid each
time.

Having made myself sick over our present condition,
I determined the minimum amount we would need in
our account for me to feel at ease about leaving on our

family trip. Acknowledging God's help in the past, I prayed for His help now. Seven-hundred dollars would be enough. The deposit the following day was $710.09.

How foolish I had been to worry, when I knew God would provide. He always does. At times we have had to borrow money; other times the mail is loaded with checks. His way of providing a solution may change, but God has never forsaken me in my time of need.

Dear Father, thank You for the rich blessings You have given me. Help me to face the times of plenty and the times of want without worry. Help me remember that You will take care of me always. Amen.

Kimberly De Jong, besides writing, enjoys counted cross-stitch, sewing, refunding, and garage sales. She's active in her women's group at school and is part-time bookkeeper in her family's print shop. Kimberly and her husband, Phil, have two children and reside in Ripon, California.

Uninvited Fear

Mary Jane Donaldson

*I will be glad and rejoice in your love, for
you saw my affliction and knew the
anguish of my soul. You have not handed
me over to the enemy but have set my feet in
a spacious place.* Psalm 31:7-8, *NIV*

Fear was my constant companion as
a child. I was bound by the fear of being alone and of
the dark.

Night coming through windows with the blinds still
open made me imagine horrible things lurking in the
shadows, waiting to enter at any opportune moment. I
was afraid to take the trash out after dark; I imagined
something hiding in the shadows ready to grab me.
Babysitting as a teen was a nightmare because of all the
strange noises I thought I heard.

My level of fear rose after I married and had
children. There were times my husband had to be out
and I would be a mental wreck if he wasn't home by ten
o'clock; by then the children were snuggled in their
beds, and the house and neighborhood were quiet and
still. Disturbing thoughts would then take over my
thought processes.

As the years passed, I was better able to reason with

myself about fear, and it did get better, but it was always there.

Recently, as our pastor closed his sermon, he asked if there were any present who had an uncontrollable problem in their life. He said to ask Jesus to show you the root of the problem and then to ask for His healing.

As I bowed by head, I remembered my constant battle with fear. "Jesus, please show me the root of the problem and heal me," I prayed.

Immediately, a scene flashed across my memory screen. I was a little girl; my brothers, sister, and I were tucked into bed for the night. My mom had gone to the movies with a neighbor, and my dad was sitting in his easy chair listening to the radio. I got up to talk to him but discovered he wasn't there. I felt frightened, unprotected, and all alone, vunerable to all the intruders I had heard adults talk about. Actually, Dad had gone to his workshop, only twenty feet from the house.

Satan set up a stronghold of fear in my life that night, which crippled me for many years. But, since that time of prayer I have been seeing the truth and the truth is setting me free. And whom the Lord sets free, will be free indeed.

Heavenly Father, expose the roots of those problems in my life that would hinder my Christian growth and service to You. Amen.

Mary Jane Donaldson has written school plays and numerous articles. Besides writing, she enjoys sewing, crafts, and reading. Mary Jane and her husband, John Terrell, have five children and make their home in Ventura, California.

Green Pastures, Valley of Death

Paula Cumming Duerr

*He maketh me to lie down in green
pastures...He restoreth my soul.*
Psalm 23:2-3, *KJV*

Light swirled at the edge of
consciousness—in and out, in and out—until sharp pain
forced me to concentrate. And when my eyes focused
again, they did not recognize the place. The man who
stitched my face was a stranger...

I was seventeen then, a new Christian returning from
a conference half a state away. There were no seat belts
in those days, and if safety glass were the rule, nobody
mentioned it. As the youngest, I rode up front with the
minister and his wife in a comfortably full car.

It was dark and wet, and the rain, which lulled me to
sleep, offered little resistance to brakes suddenly applied.
We crashed into the car ahead and my face shattered the
windshield.

Beneath bandages covering half my face were scars,
red and ugly. I'd sought to please God as never before.
Why had He rewarded me thus?

For a while I avoided unspoken questions at college.
I retreated into myself. The daily walk between buses
crossed the river, and several times I stood on the bridge

and contemplated the water. Were it not for God I'd have jumped. Instead, my brother's Navigator verse kept repeating itself in my mind: *"There hath no temptation taken you but such as is common to man. But God is faithful, who will not suffer you to be tempted above that ye are able; but will with the temptation also make a way to escape, that ye may be able to bear it"* (1 Corinthians 10:13).

In God's own way He showed me what was needed. Old attitudes and buried hurts had to go. Most of the changes were internal, but He led and I followed.

"He brought me up also out of an horrible pit, out of the miry clay, and set my feet upon a rock, and established my goings and he hath put a new song in my mouth" (Psalm 40:2-3).

That was years ago. The scars are still there, but the redness disappeared almost immediately. Every so often people ask about the scars or why I didn't lose my eye...and, if they have time, I tell them about the time when God and I went to a conference.

Dear Lord: When we walk the valley of the shadow of death, show us Your presence that we may know all is according to Your will. Amen.

Paula Cumming Duerr has had numerous articles and stories published and co-authored the book *The Culturally Deprived Child* for the state of California (Universities–Ed. Dept.). She enjoys teaching, dollmaking, history, travel, natural history, and children. Recently widowed, Paula has two grown children and resides in Gilroy, California.

God and the Bat

Shirley Eaby

What time I am afraid, I will trust in thee.
Psalm 56:3, *KJV*

Except for the streetlight, it was dark when my husband left at three in the morning to put in four hours of overtime on his job. Wearing only my nightgown, I shivered as I watched him leave the drive without closing the garage door. That open garage door meant that any creep, weirdo, burglar, or rapist driving by could see that the master of the house was away with the car.

I closed and locked the door into the house, yet I felt so vulnerable. And what of the children sleeping upstairs? I didn't want my three girls molested. The more I thought about what could happen, the more frightened I became. I moved to go up the stairs...the floorboards creaked in the darkened living room. *He was inside! Probably all week long he had watched my husband leave early, and he had waited for this moment.*

I could hardly breathe as I willed my rubbery legs to climb up the stairs to the kids. How would I protect them? Fear paralyzed my mind until I remembered the verse in Psalm 1 had recently memorized. I began reciting, "What time I am afraid, I will trust in thee."

91

Suddenly, I grasped the stair rail to keep from falling...I was so weak from the laughter that exploded within me. If I trusted God as much as I thought I did, then why was I clutching the heavy baseball bat one of my boys had left in the hall?

"Sure, when I'm scared, I'll grab a bat and say I trust You, God."

No. I'd put some action to my faith. I laid down the bat where I'd found it, turned out the light, and went to bed. It was normal for my old farmhouse to creak. I wouldn't strain to listen for footsteps. It was God, and God alone, I would trust. I relaxed...and went to sleep.

Forgive me, Father, for looking at the terrors in the darkness. Thank You for being there and for backing up Your promises. I hope I passed Your test. I need You. Amen.

Shirley Eaby has had many articles, photos, news stories, and columns published. Besides writing and reading, she enjoys photography, softball, volleyball, tennis, and backpacking. Shirley and her husband, George, have five grown children and reside in Lancaster, Pennsylvania.

Thunder Storms Declare God's Glory

Pamela Erickson

*The voice of the Lord is upon the waters; the
God of glory thunders, the Lord is over
many waters. The voice of the Lord is
powerful, the voice of the Lord is
majestic...And in His temple everything
says, "Glory!" Psalm 29:3-4,9, NASB*

We moved to southeastern Arizona
when I turned six and soon experienced our first
monsoon. The air, thick with high humidity, hung over
us, weighing heavy and dulling our thoughts and play.

Mom recognized my growing apprehension. She
invited me to sit next to her on the couch after we had
turned it to face the large picture window. We watched
the darkened clouds gather in the west and slowly
progress across the valley floor. From our vantage point
in the foothills of the Huachuca mountains, we could see
at least sixty miles across.

Giant bolts of lightning zigzagged through the
heavens drawing dramatic pictures. I had never seen
such spectacular light arc so high across miles of sky. I
scooted close to Mom.

At first, the thunder rolled in the distance, half a

minute after the lightning flash. But as the lightning moved closer, the thunder rang louder and closer in time. I trembled in fear.

Mom wrapped her arms around me and spoke gently. "We have the privilege of seeing one of God's beautiful stories unfolding. Together, we'll search for familiar characters in the clouds. Remember how we have found animals in fluffy white clouds on sunny days?"

We took turns pointing to where we anticipated the next lightning bolt would strike and laughed when it came. We counted the seconds between the lightning flash and the thunder roar to judge how much closer it drew.

"Listen to the angels' applause for the lightning show," suggested Mom, when we heard another crash of thunder. She stroked my shoulder and pressed a kiss on my forehead.

As the showers fell around us, a cool wind blew in fresh air, replacing the stifling heat and lifting the burden of the recently oppressive humidity.

Securely sitting next to Mom, I learned about the splendor of God's heaven so that I would not fear the storm, but see the beauty. Mom helped me sense God's control of nature and His divine hands at work.

Thank You, God, for refreshing rain and for dramatic storms that declare Your glory. Help me always to give You praise when I see Your handiwork. Amen.

Pamela Erickson has had numerous articles published in the secular and religious press. Pamela enjoys wood crafts, sewing, and gourmet cooking. In addition, she coordinates the annual Santa Clara Valley Christian Writers seminar. She and her husband, Roger, have two children and make their home in San Jose, California.

My Child, God's Child

Jessica Cherie Errico

*For you created my inmost being; you knit
me together in my mother's womb...All the
days ordained for me were written in your
book before one of them came to be.*
Psalm 139:13,16, *NIV*

Three months pregnant, I stood at
the top of our steep stairs. My feet seemed secure, but
my emotions teetered on the brink of despair. A
remodeling project with poor ventilation had exposed
my unborn child to noxious fumes. Worry consumed me.

*Is my baby alright? Will he be retarded? How can I
cope?* My mind groped for answers.

Modern science indicates that unborn babies are
vulnerable to environmental factors, especially irritants
that enter the placenta via the mother's bloodstream. I
was frantic about the health of the baby I carried, so I
asked my doctor about an amniocentesis test.

This procedure checks primarily for Down's
syndrome by counting the baby's chromosomes. Since a
needle is inserted into the womb to extract amniotic
fluid, there is risk of miscarriage. My doctor tried to allay
my concerns while discouraging me from having the test.

"Most likely your liver filtered the fumes you're

concerned about before they reached the baby," he said.

Nonetheless, fear continued to grip my heart, fueled by the fact that my husband's thirty-three-year-old sister has been severely handicapped since birth. Standing on the top step, a dark thought taunted me. *Just fall down the stairs and all your worry will be over. You won't have to face the "if" anymore!*

In that split second, I identified with women who have an abortion out of fear. By the grace of God, however, I chose to step away from the stairs. I chose life and not death, and the Scriptures became my assurance.

King David proclaimed an eternal truth when he wrote that God formed him in his mother's womb. God creates us and knows each of our lives completely. I needed to trust Him for the future of my unborn babe, whatever that future would entail.

The next six months passed more easily, and finally Daniel was born. He arrived with a lusty cry, and though he needed minor surgery during his first year, he is completely normal! I am so blessed by this little boy's love.

Father God, trusting You with my children hasn't been easy. Yet I know that You love them even more than I do, and that You know all that lies ahead for them. Thank You for being faithful to Your promises. Amen.

Jessica Cherie Errico has published her own book of poetry and written devotionals and articles. She enjoys singing, reading, and camping, and currently serves as secretary and worship leader for her local Women's Aglow chapter. Jessica and her husband have two small children and reside in Poulsbo, Washington.

Treasures

Marjorie K. Evans

*I rejoice at Your word, as one who finds
great treasure.* Psalm 119:162, *NKJV*

When our grandchildren were very
young, I began putting surprises in their special dresser
drawers in the guest bedroom. Each time they came,
they eagerly ran to find their treasures.

Bursting into the house on Christmas Day, Charity
(four) and Cody (six) gave big bear hugs and kisses to
their grandpa and me, then raced to the bedroom.
Almost immediately, they came running out and
chorused, "Grandma! There isn't anything in my drawer."

"What day is today?" I asked.

Together they chimed, "It's Christmas, Grandma."

"Yes, it's Jesus' birthday and a very special day, isn't
it? So today your surprises are in a special place. Would
you like to look for them? When you're close, we'll say,
'You're hot,' and when you're far away, we'll say, 'You're
cold.'"

The hunt began, and soon there were squeals of
pleasure or groans of disappointment depending on
whether the children were hot or cold.

Finally, Cody and Charity were close to the large
wooden shoes from Holland, which stood near the front

door. "You're warm...warm...warmer; now you're hot!" we cried.

Suddenly, Cody looked down at the shoes. "Charity!" he exclaimed. "Here they are. Here's my surprise and here's yours." Grinning happily they sat down to examine their treasures.

Our heavenly Father loves us and delights in giving us special treats and surprises. But many times they are not in places we expect them to be. Perhaps they're in the warm handclasp of an older person who says, "You don't know how your phone calls cheer me." Or they may be in the sweet smile of a child, or in an unexpected card or letter. And often they are found in God's Word, if we are diligent in searching them out.

Dear Lord, help me to be childlike in my eagerness to find the treasures You have for me each day. And use me to pass on treasures to others. Amen.

Marjorie K. Evans, a former teacher, has had numerous articles published. Besides writing, she enjoys swimming, traveling, and gardening. She and her husband, Ed, have a ministry to the elderly and together host a Bible study in their home. The Evans have two grown sons and make their home in Downey, California.

Little Things

Marilou Flinkman

*When I consider thy heavens, the work of
thy fingers, the moon and the stars, which
thou hast ordained; What is man, that thou
art mindful of him? and the son of man,
that thou visitest him?* Psalm 8:3-4, *KJV*

There's laundry to do, a floor to
mop, food to cook. How can I find time to do the Lord's
will?

"Go for a walk," the Lord told me.

"Sure, and the board of health will condemn my
house."

"Trust Me."

I didn't listen. Instead, I surveyed the results of two
teenagers and a husband fixing breakfast.

"Lord," I fussed, picking up cereal boxes like a
whirlwind, "it would take one of Your miracles to clean
up this mess." I started to put the milk away. "Who left
just a half-inch of milk in the carton?" I cried.
Discouraged, I decided to go for that walk—to pick up
some milk at the store.

The sun was bright and made the dewdrops on my
roses sparkle. My neighbor waved to me from her
window. *Poor Ruth*, I thought, *she never gets out.*

Impulsively, I broke off a rosebud and went to her door.

"Doesn't that smell sweet?" The old lady leaned on her walker while she drank in the scent of the rose.

"Would you like to go for a walk?"

"Why, that would be nice. I don't get out much anymore."

Slowly we made our way down the street. Ruth seemed to notice every little thing—the buds on the flowers, the leaves on the trees. "Hasn't the Lord given us a magnificent world?" She squeezed my arm and whispered, "And He still has time for you and me."

We didn't walk far and I forgot to buy any milk, but I had looked at the joy in an old woman's face and felt peace.

Dear Lord, please help me remember to take time to look up from my daily chores so that I might enjoy and share the beauty of Your creation. Amen.

Marilou Flinkman has written over seventy short stories, articles, and devotions. Besides reading and writing, she enjoys speaking to women's groups. The Flinkmans make their home in Enumclaw, Washington.

Love Never Gives Up

Betty Foley

Sing to Him a new song.
Psalm 33:3, *NASB*

I responded to the doorbell in anger,
not for the caller, but because I had been putting off
replacing the old bedroom curtains for the flowery new
ones that had been waiting many months for their debut.
I did muster up a quick smile, however, as I flung open
the door, and along with the cool gentle breeze that
greeted me, three darling young girls rushed in, all
talking at once!

"We're back again!" chirped ten-year-old Dottie, and
from twelve-year-old Marsha, "Do we have a great new
dance routine!"

Suddenly, my mind began flash-carding words, like
Bible, Jesus, Sunday School, and then plans I had made
over the past two years to explain to the girls—yes, to
visit their parents and tell them too—how Jesus loves
motorcyclists, swimmers, *and* dancers! I longed to tell
them that God wants some of their time also. I did get to
witness a little to the girls during our little tea parties each
time they came, but I felt that getting them to church was
another matter that would take more time.

Their merriment interrupted my thoughts. "We're

going into the hall to practice—then WOW! Hold onto your seat!"

I propped up the pillows, leaned back, and sighed; it was the first time I had relaxed all morning. *Today, I must plant more seeds for Jesus*, I thought.

Here they came, bursting again on the scene with smiling faces, flying braids and curls, and arms linked together. And then, they began to sing, "What a Friend we have in Jesus...all our sins and griefs to bear...What a privilege to carry..."

As many times as I had heard that beloved song in church and in convalescent homes we had visited, I experienced such joy—such relief—that these little girls cared to learn this on their own and sing it with such sparkling love. I could only nod my approval.

I didn't see any wiggling dances this time, but smiles danced on their lips. And although a few more songs were sung—rather flamboyant ones for young girls—they let me know that Saturday is our regular day for entertainment now and, well, Sunday? Sunday has been mentioned more than once lately for our day of...choir, perhaps?

Heavenly Father, what a delight each day to pray and to see what You are planning for our lives. Thank You. Amen.

Betty Foley has written articles and devotions and recently retired from newspaper work. Besides writing, she enjoys music and flowers. Betty has two grown daughters and makes her home in Bakersfield, California.

The Importance of Cuddling

Mary Francess Froese

*My voice shalt thou hear in the morning, O
Lord; in the morning will I direct my prayer
unto thee, and will look up.* Psalm 5:3, *KJV*

My little gray cat lay at my feet. No
amount of coaxing would convince her to come close
and let me pet and cuddle her. A rather strange cat, she is
always lovable from a distance: following me around,
sleeping at my feet, coming when I call. But she won't
allow me the pleasure of holding her close.

This particular morning, I lay in bed listening to the
birds and watching the morning sky meld from color to
color. A part of me was feeling very guilty because this
laziness was at the expense of my quiet hour with my
Lord. This had been happening frequently, of late. The
desire for an extra hour of sleep or just the comfort of the
warm bed kept me from my most important appointment
of the day.

Now, as I lay cajoling my cat to come closer, I could
feel the warmth of the presence of the Lord in my spirit
as He likened me to my cat.

"My child, how I yearn to draw you close and cuddle
you to My breast. I have words of love to speak to you. I
know that you love Me; I know that your desire is to

serve Me...but, for our relationship to be full and directed, you need to spend time close to Me and in My Word."

How like my Father to give such a valuable lesson in such a gentle manner. With new resolve, I determined that while I can't do much about my cat's standoffish nature, I can do something about mine.

Oh, Lord, please forgive me for holding You at arm's length. It is my desire to cuddle close and have You speak sweet words of life and instruction to me. Amen.

Mary Francess Froese has published numerous articles. She is active in her community, has been a speaker for Women's Aglow, and has led women's retreats. Mary and her husband, Allen, have two grown sons and live in Vista, California.

Like a Tree Planted

Bee DeFreitas Fulfer

*And he shall be like a tree planted by the
rivers of water, that bringeth forth his fruit
in his season; his leaf also shall not wither,
and whatsoever he doeth shall prosper.*
Psalm 1:3, *KJV*

I could think of many wonderful
Scriptures that had been of great significance in my
lifetime, but this request would limit me to the book of
Psalms. I knew of many beautiful passages, but none that
had outstandingly touched my life. Or so I had thought.

Suddenly, I remembered the first time I had
memorized a Psalm. It was Psalm 1, a rather difficult one
for a young girl of ten. I had wanted to learn it perfectly,
so I had prayed for God's help. It was then that the Holy
Spirit revealed to me that being where God wanted me
to be would mean He would take care of me just as He
would a tree planted by streams of water. I guess that's
why I always loved the song we used to sing about that
Psalm, "Just like a tree planted by the waters, I shall not
be moved."

I had been moved, literally, back and forth among a
number of foster homes as a child, but, by the time I was
ten, I was in one that wanted me to stay. My new family

105

took me to a wonderful church whose Bible school teacher had assured me that, to be planted where God wanted me, I would be cared for as part of His family.

As I recall all these things, I realize how very significant the Psalms have been to my life, especially Psalm 1. And like the tree planted by streams of water, God has brought forth fruit in me, just as His Word promised He would do.

Help me, Lord, to always be submitted to Your planting, or transplanting, wherever You want me to be. Amen.

Bee DeFreitas Fulfer enjoys reading, oil painting, and home entertaining. She serves on boards both in her church and community. She is employed selling Sunday School curriculum and books for Gospel Light Publishing. Recently widowed, Bee has one grown son and makes her home in Oxnard, California.

I Shall Again Praise Him!

Joanna Karnes Fullner

*Why are you cast down, O my soul, and
why are you disquieted within me? Hope in
God; for I shall again praise him, my help
and my God.* Psalm 43:5, *RSV*

After twelve years, the marriage was over. Counseling had been helpful to me personally, but it could not save the relationship. I had three young children, a job as a social worker, a rented house, some furnishings, a used car, and a heart full of despair. How would I manage? My soul was certainly cast down, and disquiet reigned supreme. The loneliness produced by being the only adult in the house and the responsibility of being breadwinner, decision-maker, comforter, and nurturer caused me to cry out to God in anger and disbelief. How could this have happened to me? And to my amazement, God heard my plea and delivered me from despair.

At the time, I was blind to many of God's gifts. But looking back, I realize that He was always with me. My children and I were kept healthy and safe; my job offered numerous opportunities for personal growth and advancement; the church we attended provided fellowship and support; and new confidence came as I learned to cope on my own. As I gradually let others into my life, I saw how God's love is made real through the touch of other people. And slowly, as I opened myself to receive God's love, emotional and spiritual healing took place.

And then, just as I had decided I could manage quite well on my own, a Christian man came into my life—along with his two children—closing one chapter in our lives and opening another.

Challenges still confront us, and occasionally my soul experiences disquiet. But because I know my hope is in the living God who walks with me through the struggles, I do not despair.

O Lord, help me to trust You not only in the times of struggle, but also in the times of celebration. Thank You for Your faithfulness in all of life and for being my help and my hope. Amen.

Joanna Karnes Fullner, besides writing, enjoys reading, playing the piano, and walking. She is involved in several ministries at her church, where she is on staff as "parish worker." Joanna and her husband, Richard, have five grown children and reside on Bainbridge Island, Washington.

Moving
Again?

Joy P. Gage

*Lord, thou hast been our dwelling place in
all generations.* Psalm 90:1, *KJV*

Like millions of other Americans, my
husband and I might be classified as frequent movers.
The military, the clergy, the world of corporate
business—these occupations are but a few which
demand periodic relocations.

Prior to coming to our present location, we had
broken all previous records by staying in one town (and
one house!) for almost a dozen years. When we moved, I
was at once in love with our new surroundings, but my
joy was considerably dampened by the knowledge that
this would not be permanent.

Then I met Helen. As we were moving into the
community, they were making plans to move out. Her
chaplain husband had received orders, and they had six
months left before relocation. In that short time we
became good friends. Through observing Helen, I gained

a new perspective on the frequent-mover life-style.

In the ten years that I have known Helen, she has lived in four different homes. I have visited her in all of them. In every case, her house looked as though she were planning to stay there forever. She unpacked all the treasures, hung all the family pictures, and even planted flowers. Nothing about her surroundings revealed the fact that in less than three years she would be on the move again.

On one occasion, I remarked to her, "If I knew I were going to move every two or three years, I wouldn't even unpack."

She explained that she tried to handle each move as an adventure, and then said, "I made up my mind that if Wally was going to make a career out of the military that I would make a home for us wherever we went."

Before I met Helen, I frequently justified my complaining by reminding the Lord that I wasn't asking for a fancy home, just a more permanent one. I reasoned that even the Apostle Paul identified physical hardship with the state of having "no certain dwelling-place" (1 Corinthians 4:11). Observing Helen's positive attitude caused me to reexamine my own.

While the Lord was teaching me through my friend, He also began to speak to me through my ongoing study on the life of Moses, the writer of the 90th Psalm. Moses was a man who knew many dwelling places: a slave hut, a pitch-covered basket, a palace, a shepherd's tent, and crude dwellings in the wilderness experience. While he had his share of questions and complaints, the question of dwelling places was not among them.

I have come to see that neither the house itself, nor the permanent nature of the address really matters. What matters is that God's presence is in the dwelling place.

Lord, today, I pray for all those who fall into the frequent-mover life-style. May we recognize the relative unimportance of permanent addresses and respond to the unique challenge of making a home wherever we are. Amen.

Joy P. Gage is a conference speaker and the author of seven non-fiction books. Currently working on her first novel, she is the wife of a pastor and mother of three grown daughters. Joy enjoys quilting, hiking, swimming, and traveling. She and her husband make their home in San Rafael, California.

Unchangeable

Mona Gansberg-Hodgson

But Thou art the same, and Thy years will not come to an end. Psalm 102:27, *NASB*

I was exhausted. Packing, tying up loose ends at my job, picking up immunization records from the schools, and saying good-bye had left me weary and sad.

The move to Arizona loomed before me like a mysterious shadow, hiding an unknown future. Moving wasn't so strange because we had relocated before, but this was different. We were moving out of the state of my birth. California had been my home for over thirty years.

As we loaded the last of our things into the moving van, I became acutely aware of how much our lives, circumstances, and surroundings are subject to change. A relocation leaves us no choice but to change.

We say good-bye to old friends and seek out new ones. We attend new schools, start new jobs, and find new churches.

A recent experience of helping to care for a sick grandparent reminded me that change is also an integral part of aging. Our needs and capabilities change many times during childhood and adulthood. It seems like yesterday that I was parenting toddlers, but now they are both teenagers. Throughout the growing and maturing process we face various role changes. Sometimes they include switching roles in our parent/child relationships.

I appreciate some newness and spontaneity in my life, but sometimes the changes life brings get me down, and I crave stability and sameness. When I find myself discouraged and dried by the winds of change, I turn to Psalm 102.

What an enormous comfort I find in knowing that there is One who isn't subject to change. Present in the beginning (verse 25) and enduring after all else has perished (verse 27), God is eternal. He is unchangeable. Hallelujah! He is my stability.

Lord, thank You for the assurance I find in You. Help me to lean more fully on You, my unchanging Savior. Amen.

Mona Gansberg-Hodgson has authored over one hundred devotions, articles, and poems and writes a syndicated weekly newspaper column. She enjoys tennis, camping, music, travel, and table games. Mona and her husband, Bob, have two daughters and make their home in Cottonwood, Arizona.

Don't Count Sheep

Martha E. Garrett

At midnight I will rise to give thanks unto
thee because of thy righteous judgments.
Psalm 119:62, *KJV*

During the twenty-five years I've been a Christian, I've thought of insomnia as a special gift from heaven. I was therefore quite shocked when my doctor asked me recently if I suffered from insomnia.

"I don't suffer from insomnia," I replied. "I enjoy it; that is, if you mean waking during the night and remaining sleepless for several hours. Out of the twenty-four hours in the day, those are my most delightful!"

The doctor looked at me the way a psychiatrist might look at a patient who is telling him about how he likes to take off all his clothes under Macy's Christmas tree. As he wrote insomnia under "Diseases" on the medical questionnaire, I wondered if he was thinking, "Insomnia—delightful? H-mmm? This patient needs a psychiatrist more than she needs me..."

"Doctor, I'd like to tell you why insomnia isn't a problem in my life. Those still, quiet hours in the night, when I sit at my table reading my Bible or writing in my devotional journal are wonderful. It's so peaceful, my mind is uncluttered, and I sense the Lord's presence."

The doctor cleared his throat, as he glanced at his watch. There was more I wanted to say. I wanted to tell him about the song that often went through my mind..."He walks with me; He talks with me; He tells me I am His own...." What a joy!

"Insomnia," according to Roget's Thesaurus, means "vigilant, to be wide awake, attentive, alert." I'm thankful for those wide-awake hours.

Had my doctor been willing to listen, I would have told him how God fortifies me for the day ahead with the gift of insomnia during the night. The day often gathers too much momentum and passes as a breeze, but when it's calm and peaceful "at midnight, I will rise to give thanks unto thee" (Psalm 119:62, *KJV*).

Possibly because of the refreshing time spent with my closest friend, Jesus Christ, I get quality sleep when I go back to bed. Invariably, I wake early in the morning, full of energy for the busy daylight hours ahead.

Could it be that the problem with people who suffer from insomnia is that too many lie in bed counting sheep instead of talking to the Shepherd?

O thank You that You are so available to all who love You, Jesus! Thank You that I know You and love You! Amen.

Martha E. Garrett has written numerous articles, writes hundreds of letters each year, and has kept a devotional journal for twenty years. She has four grown children and resides in East Wenatchee, Washington.

Lord, Thank You for That Rental

Wilma Brown Giesser

Offer to God a sacrifice of thanksgiving.
Psalm 50:14, *RSV*

My hands gripped the steering wheel. Anger churned in the pit of my stomach. The closer I came to our rental property, the angrier I became.

I was trying to pray, but it was a one-sided prayer; I was doing all the talking—no listening. I was telling God that we had trusted Him when we bought the rental and that we couldn't go on putting money into it. "And, Lord, if we sell it now," I added, "we'll lose all we've put into it— we'll lose all the appreciation we're hoping to make on it."

We were counting on a profit from that rental. That was part of our plans for future security. But my husband was getting tired of replacing broken windows and ruined carpet. He thought it had become a poor investment and he wanted to sell it. I was angry at him—and scared for our future.

Suddenly, I remembered a verse of Scripture: "Offer to God a sacrifice of thanksgiving." Thanksgiving? Now? For what? How was I to offer a sacrifice of thanksgiving when I didn't feel thankful?

But I began to try. I thanked God for loving me, for Jesus, for my husband and our family. I thanked Him for everything I could think of. Through thanking Him, I began to open my mind to allow Him to speak to me. Finally, I wanted to be in His will more than I wanted to have my own way.

It was at that point I could say, "Lord, thank You for that rental. We can sell it or keep it—I don't care."

My grip loosened on the steering wheel. My face relaxed. My anger was gone. I began to sing, for I was feeling great! I had come from "pity poor me" to thanking and praising God.

We did sell the rental soon after, and we did lose heavily. But I can still say, "Lord, thank You for that rental." From it we gained a deeper insight into real security, which is found only in God and His providence.

Lord, You know it isn't easy for me to want to thank You for the hurtful things in my life, but I thank You for teaching me about the power of thanksgiving. Amen.

Wilma Brown Giesser has authored numerous articles and devotionals. She enjoys traveling with her husband, reading, walking, entertaining friends, and spending time with her family. She and her husband, Don, have three grown children and make their home in Sacramento, California.

Stuck Taffy

Bernice Gomez

Search me, O God, and know my heart:
try me, and know my thoughts.
                    Psalm 139:23, *KJV*

Excitement bubbled in my head as I thought about winning another first prize. Slowly, the concoction began to boil. I was going to have the best taffy at the county fair! I took the pot off the stove and placed it on the table, where room-temperature butter and vanilla waited next to the large pastry board. As I grasped the handle of the wooden spoon to turn the taffy out onto the board, I felt resistance. Just in a matter of seconds the taffy had hardened; I couldn't even move the spoon. I fought with the pot and spoon handle, trying to pry out the taffy. It wouldn't budge. I mean, like, "Nix to you, kid, no way!"

"Check the ingredients," my mind raced. "What did you forget? Check!" As I took inventory, I noted nothing was missing. Quickly, I checked my recipe book for other taffy recipes: Vinegar! The missing ingredient was vinegar. I didn't have enough time to make more because I had to meet the Monday morning deadline with my other finished entries.

Despite my setback, however, there was a grin on my

face all that day, for the experience had brought back memories of the hardest time of my life—a time when I felt as stuck as that mess of taffy. I had had back surgery and I was in constant pain. Eventually, depression set in. Stuck! There was no way I wanted to live. People had no meaning. Time had stopped. Half hours became days. "God, where are You? Let me die!" Still pain.

But then there was a breakthrough after fourteen months. Just as I had declared my winnings at the fair, I affirmed, "I am going to win over this thing!" God's grace brought me "vinegar." And with it came the victory! My prize—learning to overcome pain—was better than any blue ribbon I had ever won. And I'm still winning today, thanks to God's grace.

Dear Lord, help me to not give up on You when I am in pain. Cause me to come to You to receive Your sweet comfort. Amen.

Reverend Bernice Gomez, besides writing, enjoys sewing, baking, and floral design. She serves as the only woman on the bi-lingual ministerial board for her locality. She and her husband, John, have five children and make their home in Oxnard, California.

Mother's Shepherd

Bonnie S. Grau

The Lord is my shepherd; I shall not want.
Psalm 23:1, *KJV*

Recently, I had the privilege of spending a weekend with my mother who, several years ago, had moved to a retirement village some sixty miles away from our hometown. Since that move, our visits have not been frequent, but they have had a quality of togetherness that "pop-in" calls often lack. This last one was no exception, as we enjoyed dinner with family friends, visits to several of Mother's new friends, a best-out-of-five Scrabble tournament...and a special walk.

As we made our way along her usual route, she pointed out the homes of other residents, as well as a garden from which she had been given an open invitation to take fresh vegetables. Then we left the path and followed a meandering stream. After crossing a little bridge, we sat down on a bench.

"Sometimes I say the Twenty-third Psalm out loud when I sit here," Mother said. "It seems to go with this place."

Mother turned eighty on her last birthday. As I sat there, I thought of how she had walked with the Shepherd for most of that time, and how He had led her to green pastures and still waters. And on that day when she would walk through the valley of the shadow of death, she would not be afraid, for she knew that He would not desert her there.

My thoughts wandered on to my own two daughters. What better legacy could I leave them than that which my mother is leaving me? All of the right things I've tried to do as a mother and all of the material things I've given them could not begin to compare with the assurance they would have of knowing that their mother walked with the Shepherd. I hoped that not only did they already have that assurance, but that they would desire to leave the same legacy to their own children.

Thank You, Lord, for a godly mother and for the example she has set for me. As I live before my daughters, may they see the Shepherd and desire to live their lives for Him. Amen.

Bonnie S. Grau has written several articles and writes a weekly feature article for a local newspaper. She enjoys reading, music, travel, and photography. Bonnie and her husband have two grown daughters and reside in Marysville, Pennsylvania.

Blind Eyes Made to See

Carol Green

*The Lord is my shepherd, I shall not want;
he makes me lie down in green pastures. He
leads me beside still waters; he restores my
soul...Surely goodness and mercy shall
follow me all the days of my life; and I shall
dwell in the house of the Lord for ever.*
Psalm 23:1-3,6, *RSV*

"The Lord is my shepherd...the
Lord is my shepherd...the Lord is my shepherd..." Those
words tumbled through my mind, round and round, as I
sank deeper into sleep. When I woke from this last eye
surgery—one of many—I felt the warm, firm grip of my
husband's hand. He stood at my side, my flesh-and-
blood shepherd.

"He makes me lie down in green pastures." *No, not
here in the hospital.* The doctor's kind but strong voice
penetrated my darkness. "Remember, you must lie face
down, not turning your head to either the right or the
left." My husband squeezed my hand as if to say, "You
can do it." But could I? For how long? Four, maybe six
weeks?

"He leads me beside still waters." *No, not here in the
hospital.* The nurses, some with heavy footsteps, others

with lighter footsteps, came and checked and rechecked my IV or fastened and unfastened my blood-pressure cuff.

Stillness at last. My husband had left. *The nurses must be on a coffee break.* I thought, *will my sight be restored?* In the silence, the words, "He restores my soul" slipped into the quiet and I fell asleep.

My sight wasn't restored. Months went by and I learned to walk with a white cane and I struggled with Braille. My husband encouraged me with many hugs, saying, "You can do it."

But when the frustration of not being able to find something or the sadness of not seeing the faces of my children overwhelm me, I feel the strong gentle hands of the Lord. He is holding my aching heart; "I am your Shepherd, you shall not want."

Thank You, Father, for sending me a flesh-and-blood shepherd to guide me and to hold my hand. When my path is too difficult and too dark, thank You for carrying me through the shadows into Your precious sunlight. Amen.

Carol Green, besides writing, enjoys artwork and exhibits, theater and concerts. She is a co-leader of a Bible study group and plans women's retreats. Carol and her husband, Richard, have three grown children and reside in Walnut Creek, California.

An Open and Shut Case

Lois Ellen Hall

Set a guard, O Lord, over my mouth;
keep watch over the door of my lips.
Psalm 141:3, *NASB*

This week, when a friend was late meeting me at a designated time and place to complete a church task, I had several opportunities to vent my feelings by telling others of her failure and laxity. But each time the opportunity came to degrade her, the Lord reminded me to keep silent.

My friend finally arrived and explained that she had completely forgotten about our appointment. She humbly apologized. What a relief to know that I had not uttered unkind words against her.

Often I have said, "Why, oh, why, can't I learn to keep my mouth shut? What I need is a gag over my mouth!"

But instead of a gag, I wonder what would happen if we had thought detectors to pass through, just as there are metal detectors in airports for security. Can you visualize thought detectors somehow able to screen our minds for unacceptable thoughts? Critical thoughts, which produce bitter attitudes, could be discarded before any grumbling, gossip, or slander could be uttered.

The Holy Spirit is like a thought detector, checking our spirits with His still small voice.

The Psalmist asked the Lord to set a guard over his mouth and to keep watch over the door of his lips. I will do the same and more. I want the Holy Spirit to check unacceptable thoughts before they even get a chance to reach my lips.

Please, dear Lord, forgive me when I take control of my life and seek to get even with others by saying hurtful things against them. Thank You for the faith to believe that You will check my thoughts before I hurt others with unkind words. Amen.

Lois Ellen Hall, besides writing, enjoys china painting, reading, water aerobics, Bible study, and Christian fellowship. She and her husband, Bill, have three grown children and make their home in Boise, Idaho.

Let It Snow!

April Hamelink

Purify me with hyssop, and I shall be clean;
Wash me, and I shall be whiter than snow.
Psalm 51:7, *NASB*

It's snowing. Pure, white loveliness drifts like a dancer, wrapping the world in quiet. Our yard is covered in softness, untouched and clean. My littlest one snuggles down a little deeper into my lap, and she and I experience the magical peace this moment brings.

But not for long. Soon our yard is full of laughing, rosy-cheeked children, yelling and throwing snowballs. The quiet and peace are replaced by fat snowmen in funny hats and snow forts as high as a child's reach. The baby goes down for a nap and I begin to sort through the mountain of laundry that wet weather seems to bring. All of a sudden, the snow doesn't seem all that special anymore; it's just the cause of more work.

God's love can be viewed like snow. When we first experience it, it is beautiful and pure, and we are filled with a sense of wonder and peace. And then, like children stomping on the just-fallen flakes, we trample and muddy that purity with sin, and the holiness of God's love loses some of its beauty for us.

How do I keep the wonder and peace that I first felt upon knowing God and still muddle through the slush of everyday life? The answer, of course, is that I can't. But God can, as I allow Him to purify me and make me clean, to wash me and make me whiter than snow. A cleansing from God can last even through dirty laundry and willful children, through all the grubbiness of life.

He gives us snowfalls and quiet moments to remind us of the reality of unmerited grace, of the practicality of hope. And He continues to add clean snow to our lives to renew us, refreezing and reshaping us as it pleases Him. He takes the commonness of life and makes of it something uncommonly wonderful.

Only sometimes, I forget and focus on myself. It's then that He sends another snowflake of unequalled beauty...and I remember God.

Dear Father, thank You for the moments of magic that remind me of what You're doing in my life. Cover the mud and slush, that I make, with the new and continued snowfall of Your grace. Amen.

April Hamelink, besides writing, enjoys reading to children, collecting children's books, teaching Sunday School, and delivering children's sermons put to music. April and her husband, Pete, have two children and reside in Port Orchard, Washington.

Making Decisions

Beverly Hamilton

*The steps of a man are established by the
Lord; and He delights in his way. When he
falls, he shall not be hurled headlong;
because the Lord is the One who holds
his hand.* Psalm 37:23-24, *NASB*

"I don't know what to do," I sighed
to my friend Mildred. "What if I change jobs and the new
one doesn't work out?"

Mildred answered, "But if this new job does offer you
quick advancements, you'll be sorry if you don't take
it...don't you think?"

I hate making decisions. What if I make the wrong
choice? It doesn't matter if the decision is large or small,
it's almost impossible for me to make up my mind. I've
been like this all my life. Should I get married...or not?
Should I work after marriage...or stay home? Is one baby
going to be lonely...or are three better...or four? Now I'm
asking, "Should I change jobs...or stick it out in a dead-
end position?"

I even try to get friends and relatives to make
decisions for me. But they're too wise to let me off the
hook that easily. I have to do it myself.

Even though I spend time in prayer and search the

Scriptures, no miraculous answers appear in the sky over my house at high noon. When I follow the time-proven method of listing pros and cons, I come up with just as many answers for not doing something as I do for taking action. Sometimes it seems hopeless, yet I don't believe God wants me to spend my brief days on earth anguishing over what to do or what not to do.

Recently, I read in the Scriptures, "When he falls..." *When* he falls. God knows we are not perfect; He knows we will make wrong decisions from time to time. And when we do, Scripture goes on to say that He's right there with us, holding our hands through it all.

I remember when I was a little girl and my earthly father would hold my hand as we crossed the street. He did that to protect me. I smile as I picture God with me on my journey through life, and I know that no matter what decision I make in the matter of changing jobs, or anything else, He is right there beside me, holding my hand.

Father, thank You for the freedom I have in my life. You provide so many opportunities from which to choose and You hold my hand as I make my decisions. Amen.

Beverly Hamilton has written articles for a variety of magazines. She enjoys quilting, sailing, reading, and biking. Beverly and her husband have four grown children and make their home in Fullerton, California.

God's Love and a Green Balloon

Donna Hamilton

*I lift up my eyes to the hills—where does my
help come from? My help comes from the
Lord, the Maker of heaven and earth.*
Psalm 121:1-2, *NIV*

As we were walking across the
parking lot, a tug of breeze pulled Christy's balloon and
the string snapped. Her bright green balloon danced
upward and away, over the hilltops.

Our two-year-old daughter's cries filled the air. "My
green b'loon! My green b'loon!" On the journey home,
her sobs continued.

I tried to cheer her by making up a story about her
"green balloon's trip." Paul, her teenaged brother, told
her we'd get her another one, sometime.

But the only one she seemed to listen to was six-year-
old Torrey, "You'll get it back later, Christina, 'cause the
air goes out of those and they go down, so you'll get it
back at home, Christina."

As we sped past hill after hill, I silently prayed, "Lord,
what are the chances of a balloon landing in the yard of
the people who lost it—twelve miles away?" I wanted to
ask Him to take it there, but couldn't; it was too fantastic
for my faith.

Torrey's assurance continued, "You'll get it back at home, Christina."

As we parked, Christy's little voice was excited, "My b'loon home!" We set her on the walk; she hurried to the door, "My b'loon home!"

"Look at that! She thinks her balloon is here! She thinks it blew home." I was trying to think how to soften the second blow.

We opened the door, and she rushed into the house, looking around. We all saw it at the same time. There was a green balloon under the telephone table!

Certainly it was darker than the other one, not as large either, but Christy didn't notice. "My b'loon home!" she shrilled.

"Mom, where did that come from?" Amazement was in Paul's voice.

I didn't know then; later, I recalled Christy had gotten a balloon at a wedding over two weeks before. How it survived and got in that particular, visible spot without being noticed earlier I don't know. But I do know, even a little sparrow is not forgotten before God (Luke 12:6), and I believe the sorrow of a little girl who's lost her "green b'loon" does not escape His great notice either.

Lord, I praise You! Grant me a child's faith to look not at the impossibility of a situation, but to trust You, knowing that Your ability and willingness to meet needs are far beyond my small vision. Amen.

Donna Hamilton is a regular contributor to the *Chapelonian* and has published some of her poetry. She is a speaker at prayer workshops, conferences, and Aglow meetings, and teaches women's Bible studies. Donna and her husband, Ed, have five children and reside in Chino, California.

The Wideness of God's Mercy

Freya Ottem Hanson

*You broaden the path beneath me, so that
my ankles do not turn.* Psalm 18:36, *NIV*

"Your brother needs your help this
summer," my mother told me. "You can help him walk."

The doctor had set the dates for my ten-year-old
brother's foot surgeries. Two surgeries would be
necessary to correct his turned and twisted feet. Then he
would have to be in casts for the entire summer. But, if
the surgeries were successful, his feet would be straight,
and he would walk with fewer sprained ankles.

So I helped! I carried my brother's crutches to him. I
carried toys outdoors so he could play. I lifted him up
when he fell. I brought him Kool-Aid and Popsicles.
Even after he was more adept at getting around on his
crutches, I continued to meet his demands for help.

I, his younger sister, was asked in those hot weeks of
summer, to broaden a path for my brother so he could
stand and walk again. It was my privilege.

As children of the Almighty, our God also broadens
our paths and mercifully forgives us so we can stand and
walk in His light. He sent a Savior to cover our sins with
His love. "Oh, the depth of the riches of the wisdom and
knowledge of God! How unsearchable his judgments,

and his paths beyond tracing out!" (Romans 11:33). Again and again, our gracious God picks us up, restores our lives, and sends us on our way.

As we mirror the breadth of God's mercy, we are also called to widen the path of mercy for others. Not to judge or to condemn or to cast away, but "to bind up the brokenhearted" (Isaiah 61:l), take them by the hand, and lead them home.

That summer of my childhood was a hot, demanding one, but my brother walked again, and this time his ankles did not turn.

Thank You, Lord, for broadening the path to include me—yes, me. Help me show the broadness of that mercy to others in everything I do and say. Amen.

Freya Ottem Hanson has had numerous articles and devotions published and has authored one book. She is an attorney and a member of the Minnesota Christian Writers Guild. Freya enjoys calligraphy, piano, and teaching. She and her husband, John, have one son and make their home in New Brighton, Minnesota.

Words of Strength

Dorothy M. Harpster

Even though I walk through the valley of the
shadow of death, I will fear no evil, for you
are with me; your rod and your staff, they
comfort me. Psalm 23:4, *NIV*

"You have a problem," were the
words my sister-in-law heard when she answered the
phone shortly after Christmas. Anne had been given
tests, and her fears were realized when she was informed
that cancer cells had been found in her uterus.

This was the second time she'd received this kind
of news. Several years before, she'd had a mastectomy.
Now the doctor was telling her she'd need many
radiation treatments, after which there would be
surgery.

As I went with Anne to the hospital for her second
treatment, we met an attractive, pleasant-faced woman
coming out. She smiled and said something about "us
sick people." I told her she didn't look ill.

"You don't either," she assured us, then added
cheerfully, "We won't give up, will we?" With that, she
walked quickly and confidently to her car.

I was grateful we'd met at just that time. What a
blessing she was, for she had the secret for the ill

person's peace and the will to overcome in the fearful and uncertain times of life.

We won't give up are words of strength and courage, of determination to do one's part in the healing process. This is especially meaningful for the patient who puts complete trust in God and commits her whole situation to Him.

Anne has that kind of faith. She trusts God completely, knowing He's sufficient for all her needs, now and forever. She completed her radiation treatments, had her surgery, and has been free of cancer for several years.

I sometimes wonder how much of the courage she's displayed was a result of hearing that one wise woman's remark.

Dear Heavenly Father, may I always remember that You are with me. Help me to commit myself to Your love and care and to assist others going through difficult times. Amen.

Dorothy M. Harpster, a retired elementary school teacher, enjoys writing, traveling, classical music, reading, and educational lectures. In addition, Dorothy is active in church work and belongs to a writers group. She resides in Watsontown, Pennsylvania.

Beauty for Ashes

Allegra Harrah

Be still, and know that I am God.
Psalm 46:10, *KJV*

I listened to the young people that were crowded into the large tent, singing in many languages. Their songs were filled with praise to God. We were in Helsinki, Finland, for a European Youth for Christ Conference.

My heart was touched with God's love through those young people, and I recalled a verse that meant so much to me. In Isaiah 61:3, God says that He will give us beauty for ashes, the oil of joy for mourning, and a garment of praise for a spirit of heaviness that we might be called oaks of righteousness.

As I listened to those young people sing, I remembered the time when we had settled in Heidelberg, Germany. So many things needed to work out, and, at times, the pressures were overwhelming. It felt like ashes!

When we arrived, there was no established Youth for Christ work—no office, no staff. There was no housing available for our family. We were told that the military school we wanted our children to attend was crowded and that our children would not be accepted because we were not military. An edict had gone out from the Seventh Army headquarters that no parachurch organization could minister on a base. The list of impossibilities went on and on.

We searched our hearts. Had we missed God's guidance? But as we went back over all the details, we knew we were where we should be. God gave me the verse from Psalms, "Be still, and know that I am God."

In time, God indeed gave beauty for ashes. For, eventually, we had a beautiful home, the children were accepted in school with no problems, and God let us watch Him do a marvelous work with Youth for Christ, as He placed Christians in strategic places and opened ways where there had previously been no doors. There were rallies, school assemblies, church services, retreats, and conferences, and many came to receive Jesus as Lord and Savior. His beauty had replaced my ashes, and my cold heart was warmed by His love.

I began to sing now with the youth, and as I joined hands with those next to me, my soul swelled with praise for the One who gives beauty for ashes.

Dear Father, thank You that when I felt everything crumbling around me, You gave beauty for ashes. Quiet my heart today. May I feel Your arms around me and Your hand holding mine. Amen.

Allegra Harrah is the author of *Prayer Weapons*. She teaches Bible classes and speaks at conferences and retreats. Allegra enjoys baking and music. She and her husband, Cal, are publishers of Harrah House Ministries. The Harrahs have eight grown children and reside in Redlands, California.

Accepting a Precious Gift

Mary Harris

For the redemption of their soul is precious.
Psalm 49:8, *KJV*

When I was six years old, I discovered an antique lavaliere amid the tangled contents of my mother's jewelry box. Even at that unsophisticated age, I recognized quality and plucked it from the collection of costume jewelry.

Immediately, I fell in love with its delicate design. Gold filigree framed a carved flower in the raised center of the pendant. A tiny diamond sparkled from the middle of the petals and a seed pearl dangled from the bottom.

Without considering that it belonged to my mother or might be valuable, I took the lavaliere to my friend Linda's house. We spent the afternoon playing with our dolls in her bedroom. At dinnertime, we hurriedly cleaned up our mess before I went home. In my haste, I left the lavaliere under Linda's bed, where it lay until her mother found it while cleaning.

Guessing its value, her mother was horrified to find that the upraised floral center had been crushed under the bed's casters. After asking Linda who owned it, Mrs. Gardner brought the pendant to my mother.

"Mary, did you take this out of my jewelry box?" Mom asked me after Mrs. Gardner left. I nodded. Then I noticed the damage. My heart sank as I expected the worst.

My mother didn't punish me. Instead, she explained about the real value of the lavaliere. It probably wasn't worth much money, but it had great sentimental value. It had been a gift to my maternal grandmother, who had given it to my mother when she was old enough to appreciate it. Mom had intended to pass it on to her first daughter, me. Now, I abandoned hope of ever possessing it; I thought I would never deserve such a gift.

When I graduated from high school, my parents gave me a typewriter. My grandmother's two sisters handed me a small box. To my astonishment, it contained the lavaliere, restored, polished, and suspended from a fine chain. Dismissing my earlier folly, Mom had asked my great-aunts to repair the lavaliere as their gift to me.

Now that I am older, I regard the lavaliere in a new light. It is like the gift of truth our heavenly Father presents to us, giving us the opportunity to accept its value. Even though we are not worthy, He does not reject us or revoke his offering. He waits until we understand and accept Him.

I treasure the lavaliere and the lesson it taught me. One day I will pass it on to my daughter, if I have one, or my first granddaughter. But I have another gift to share, my legacy of faith. I pray my children will choose to inherit this precious gift and be mindful of its great value.

Lord, thank You for paying the price for my redemption. May the reminder of Your gift bring me closer to You and serve to enhance my faith. Amen.

Mary Harris has published poems and articles. She is the president of the Simi Valley, California, branch of the National League of American Pen Women, and enjoys needlework and photography. Mary and her husband, Gary, have one son and live in Simi Valley.

Place of Refuge

Marsha-Marie Clayton Harry

*Trust in Him at all times, you people; Pour
out your heart before Him; God is a refuge
for us. Selah.* Psalm 62:8, *NKJV*

Escaping for a week to the Big
Island of Hawaii was a dream come true. I was free
from a daily schedule crammed with demands upon
my time and emotions.

Sitting on a low, stone wall, listening to the waves
breaking against the warm sand released a tightness
within me. As I breathed in the peace and quiet around
me, the sound of tourists laughing and talking startled
me out of my reverie. Just then, an energetic guide
bounced into sight, closely followed by his little group
of sightseers. They huddled around him as he began to
weave his tale of this part of the island.

According to his story, this area was called the City
of Refuge, because it was a sanctuary for natives who
had escaped from enemies or who had accidentally
killed someone. Here they found protection and
shelter.

I could visualize a grassy hut with a frightened soul
lying exhausted upon a mat, terrified, too weary to
move. I was a kindred spirit with these refugees of old,

for I, too, have often sought a place of refuge, a place I could run to and hide from my enemies.

Where does one go to escape the pressures of this world? Women today have a constantly changing and often uncertain role. Where do we go to find answers to daily problems? Whom do we ask concerning the mistakes of the past, the actions of the present, and the direction for the future? These constant dilemmas are our present-day accusers.

I have found God to be my constant refuge. He is unchanging, always accessible, always loving. I can pour out my heart to Him every morning and He becomes my strength for the day, as He fills me with His positive power and nature.

I can seek Him at noontime to empower me with His directive Spirit. He leads me through whatever destructive darkness my enemies have set before me.

As I lie upon my bed at night, I can call out to Him. I can trust Him to calm my fears and frustrations and hide me under His protective covering.

In Him I can become more of the woman He designed me to be. When I accepted Jesus Christ as the Son of God, He kept His promise to become my refuge in this life.

Dear Heavenly Father, thank You for not being a temporary refuge, but an everlasting stronghold. Thank You for surrounding me with Your love and strength for each part of the day. Thank You for being always accessible to me, Your daughter. Thank You for Your unquestionable love. Amen.

Marsha-Marie Clayton Harry writes devotionals, short stories, and poetry. She enjoys sailing, painting, collecting antiques, traveling, and speaking. Marsha-Marie is a teacher and makes her home in Newbury Park, California.

A Broken Mold

Eileen Hegel

I run in the path of your commands,
for you have set my heart free.
Psalm 119:32, *NIV*

I used to sit and watch the other girls as they played in their pink satin dresses and patent leather shoes, their finely curled silk tresses blowing gracefully in the wind. Even then, I knew that wasn't me. I liked wearing my baseball glove and high-topped tennis shoes, so I could play rough with the boys. It never bothered this kid.

As I grew older, people began to tell me how I "should act." So, I tried to change, to fit into the "perfect woman" mold. However, there was one problem: I didn't fit. Oh, sure, on the outside I looked great, but I had to bury my true self, as I pretended to be someone everyone else wanted me to be.

Once, when I was out on a date, my escort said, "You're the toughest person I know." I thought, *I sure don't feel that way on the inside. As a matter of fact, I feel extremely sensitive.* But I couldn't tell him that.

In the next few weeks, I was determined to find some answers from God; I had so many questions about the real me. He began the process of allowing me to find my heart by first showing me I didn't have to masquerade. After all, He knew all about my cover. Through His gentle ways, I've learned to know and like myself—the one whom God created. I can be strong, but tender, too. It's okay to put on my baseball glove and high-topped tennis shoes and play rough with the boys. In fact, recently I've joined a coed softball team.

Thank You, Lord, for uncovering my heart. Use me to help others see the beauty that You have created in them. Amen.

Eileen Hegel has written numerous poems and articles. She enjoys music, sports, and art. Previously, Eileen cohosted two radio programs for women in the San Francisco area. In addition, she has designed her own line of handcrafted cards and calendars. Eileen makes her home in Pleasant Hill, California.

Please Don't Leave Me

Carolyn Henderson

But you, O Lord, be not far off; O my
Strength, come quickly to help me.
Psalm 22:19, *NIV*

"Watch me! Watch me!" yelled my active five-year-old, as he jumped into our backyard pool. After each jump he would pull himself up onto the pink cement and then jump in again. The cool water didn't dampen his enthusiasm to perfect each jump. Jon would pull himself out of the water, straighten himself as though preparing for an Olympic dive, and yell, "Watch this one!"

At first, I was afraid Jon would get hurt, but with each successful jump, I relaxed...until I heard him scream with pain. As he held his face, blood ran between his small fingers. On his last jump, he had twisted his body around and cut the soft skin under his right eye on the cement edge of the pool. I called frantically to my husband, feeling myself panicking.

We wrapped Jon in some towels and drove to the nearest emergency room. The doctor surveyed the cut and said it would require seven stitches. While Jon continued to cry in protest, the nurse wrapped him in a cloth garment with Velcro closures that immobilized his arms.

Jon was lying helpless on the hospital bed looking at me when the doctor asked me to leave the room. He said, "Mothers have been known to faint when their children are in pain."

I prayed, "Oh, Lord, be my Strength so that I can be strong for Jon." In a strong voice, I turned to the doctor and refused to leave, promising that I would not get in the way. The doctor looked at me for a few silent moments as though weighing my promise; then he agreed.

I moved to my son's bedside and reached out to hold his still, small fingers as they protruded from the "straight-jacket" that confined him. Once he felt my touch, his sobbing stopped and his breathing returned to normal. By the time the doctor was putting in the last stitch, he and Jon were discussing future Olympic jumps.

Comparing my life to Jon's experience, I realize that I too can go through any crisis when I know my Lord is nearby to hold my hand. At times I've felt that the stresses of life have kept me bound like a straight-jacket. But the Lord is there holding my hand and promising to set me free.

Lord Jesus, help me to remember that You are never far off. Help me to relax and receive Your strength. Amen.

Carolyn Henderson, besides writing, enjoys art and quilting. She is a graphic designer by profession and volunteers her time to work with victims of crime. She and her husband have three children and reside in Newbury Park, California.

We Had to Go Back

Daisy Hepburn

Lord, who may dwell in your sanctuary?
Who may live on your holy hill?....[He or
she] who keeps his oath even when it hurts.
Psalm 15:1,4, *NIV*

Following the borrowed pickup truck my husband was driving, I tried to heed his instructions to honk three times if there was any kind of an emergency. This was an emergency!

After two or three miles of honking, David finally pulled over.

"One of the rubbish bags fell off the truck a couple of exits back!" I shouted to him out my car window. "It was probably just some old linens." Then I argued, "Let's not go back. I just want to get home."

David insisted we go back, however, so we turned around and tried to locate the missing bag.

Can you picture, along the freeway, trees bedecked with pink fluff from bed pillows, and shrubbery draped with bed sheets! I pulled over and sat laughing while my husband collected our belongings before anyone we knew happened by.

Soon a stranded motorist approached my car and expressed relief that help had arrived. He said that his van had come to an abrupt halt when it ran over a plastic bag, which was now firmly affixed to the underside of his vehicle, cutting his gas tank and causing other damage to his van. Immediately, we owned up to our responsibility.

The bid on his repair work arrived later. For what we paid to have his van repaired, we could have redecorated our bedroom several times over with new linens! Why did we have go to back?

"Thank you for your good faith," the motorist said as we wrote the check to cover the damage to his van.

"Good faith," I argued with my old nature! "Lots of people drop things on the freeway and never even know it. Why did we have to go back? Why, the guy could probably have just turned the damage in to his own insurance company." Sometimes, it hurts to accept responsibility.

"Lord, who shall dwell in Your sanctuary?"

"He who keeps his oath even when it hurts."

Lord, I am counting on Your promise that by keeping Your laws there is great reward. Please help me to accept my responsibilites. Amen.

Daisy Hepburn is a frequent conference and seminar speaker and author of several books including *Glorious Living, Look, You're a Leader!*, and *Life With Spice* Bible studies. Daisy and her husband, David, have two grown children and make their home in San Francisco, California.

The Tie
That Binds

Ethel Herr

Let all the people say "Amen."
Praise the LORD! Psalm 106:48, *NASB*

Their Hindu culture called them
outcasts and treated them like untouchables. But as I
looked at the beautiful people sitting on mats in the
thatched-hut church in the coconut groves of southern
India, I knew I sat in the presence of God's special
children.

To the accompaniment of a variety of hand drums
and other rhythmic instruments, the little band of
believers sang in their native Mallayalum, with a highly
contagious enthusiasm.

Each song had a dozen stanzas, and the melodies
were distinctly Indian. But as my missionary friend and I
sat in our seats of honor looking over the jubilant
congregation, we felt a kinship that defied linguistic
barriers, or Hindu labels, and made us one.

Then the unexpected happened. I began hearing two
familiar words repeated in an enticing refrain. Irresistibly,
I found myself singing along, "Amen, Alleluia! Amen,
Alleluia!"

Alleluia, indeed. We were united by two simple
words, the only words shared by every language on

149

earth. And they were addressed to God Himself. Could it be that God had planned it this way so that we might be reminded that unity in the Body of Christ is possible not through dialogue or study or even cooperative projects, but only as we come together in our worship of Him? I remembered the vast choirs of the book of Revelation, all gathered around the throne of the Lamb, singing to Him for all eternity, "Amen, Alleluia!"

And I rejoiced to realize that the time will come when no barriers of time or space or human limitations will keep us apart. We shall all be a part of heaven's great eternal choir. The Psalmist's prayer will be answered in full, and heaven and earth will join hands to "Let all the people [with outcasts embraced as equals] say 'Amen.' Praise the LORD!" Alleluia!

Dear Heavenly Father, thank You for Your numberless family, all united in the one thing we can share in common, even on this earth, words of praise to You. Amen, Alleluia!

Ethel Herr has written numerous books and articles. She is a free-lance writer, writing instructor, and frequent conference speaker. Ethel enjoys bicycling, sewing, cooking, studying history, and reading. She and her husband, Walt, have three grown children and live in Sunnyvale, California.

Coming Home
for
Thanksgiving

Barbara Hibschman

*Let us come before His presence with
thanksgiving.* Psalm 95:2, *NASB*

It was the first Thanksgiving since we
had moved far away from Dad, who lived alone. It was
an untraditional Thanksgiving because we weren't going
home. My seminary-student husband, Jim, had a research
paper to do.

We were saddened to get a phone call on
Thanksgiving Eve telling us that Dad would be spending
the holiday alone. My only brother, Stephen, a soldier at
Fort Benning, Georgia, had a forty-eight-hour pass but
couldn't get a flight.

We hung up and exchanged looks and comments of
disappointment.

"If we could get a flight out of here and back in the
same day, or early the next morning, I could still get this
paper done," Jim reasoned.

"Tomorrow is Thanksgiving Day. Do you think we
can still get a flight? And, if we could, do we have the
money?"

"I think so, but it will have to be a big part of our
Christmas," he suggested.

"Let's go for it," I agreed.

We did get a flight, and, to our amazement, we were packed and off to the airport within a couple of hours.

We arrived early in the morning, our hearts bursting with thankfulness for how it had all worked out. We began to make preparations for the meal, but an unexpected phone call from my brother urged us to hurry back to the airport. He had spent the night in Atlanta, waiting on standby. He, too, was coming home.

Because of all the traveling, the menu was not the traditional dinner with all the trimmings, but no one minded. We were simply grateful to be together. Dad was so pleased, for he knew his children had made every effort to be with him.

God, our heavenly Father, longs for His children to "come home" and fellowship with Him too. How it must please Him when we make every effort to gather as brothers and sisters in Christ, to enjoy His presence in praise and worship. How it must delight His heart to hear expressions of thanksgiving coming from our hearts.

Dear Father, thank You that I can always come home to enjoy Your presence. Help me make every effort to be with You, so I can become more like You. Amen.

Barbara Hibschman has published over 100 articles, short stories, and poems. She enjoys singing, playing the piano, traveling, reading, and counted cross-stitch. She is a former missionary to the Philippines and speaks at women's retreats. Barbara and her husband, Jim, of Warren, New Jersey, have two children.

Camping Out

Ellen Hird

The angel of the Lord encamps around
those who fear him, and he delivers them.
Psalm 34:7, *NIV*

It was after eleven. High fog covered the night sky and a bone-chilling wind had been blowing for hours. Though I was snug in my bed, I couldn't sleep. My eyes started reading a book about angels, but my ears listened for rain.

Normally, I don't pay much attention to the weather, but that night my ten-year-old daughter was camping out on the ridge with the Girl Scouts. I kept telling myself not to worry and reminded myself that I had nagged her into taking a parka, a knitted hat, an extra pair of socks, and long pants.

"She'll be warm enough," I said finally, nestling deeper into my own covers. Then it hit me. What about the others? Not every girl is blessed with a nagging mother.

My eyes were drawn to the page in front of me. It said in 2 Kings 6:14-17 that Elisha and his servant were surrounded and protected by hosts of God's angels. An outlandish possibility tiptoed into my mind.

"Father," I prayed, "could You please send a host of

angels to surround the Girl Scouts' camp? I know that if Your angels surrounded the camp, they could keep out the cold. And would You tell them to breathe the warmth of Your love on the girls? Oh, Father, I know my request doesn't make 'grown-up' sense, but I still believe You could do it. Amen."

The next day, when I picked up my daughter, I asked her leaders, "Was it terribly cold up there last night?"

"Oh, no," said one of them. "I got up around twelve o'clock, and, it's funny, it was just toasty."

"It was almost warm," volunteered another, "not like earlier in the evening when the wind blew, and it was so cold."

My mouth dropped open in awe and thanksgiving. God had answered my "outlandish" prayer.

We Christians are all camping out in this world. The chilling winds of trouble, pain, and sorrow blow all around the flimsy tents of our lives, but we are still protected. God encircles us with Himself and warms us with His everlasting love.

Remind us, Father, that we always live within the circle of Your protection, at the center of Your love. Amen.

Ellen Hird is a volunteer for the Crisis Pregnancy Center in her area. She enjoys drawing and watercolor. Ellen is married and has one daughter. The Hirds make their home in Hayward, California.

Walk With Me, Lord!

Darlene Hoffa

*Teach me to do Thy will, for Thou art
my God.* Psalm 143:10, *NASB*

My elderly neighbor, Jenny, shuffled down the street toward me. Her hands were plunged deeply into the pockets of her shabby sweater. She peeked out from beneath her old hat, glancing from side to side.

"Oh, no!" I whispered. "Morris is missing again."

Each spring, Jenny's cat, Morris, disappears. Every time, Jenny declares him permanently vanished. She then scours the neighborhood, wrapped in a cloak of despondence. Today, Jenny acted more depressed than ever.

"Hi, friend," I greeted her. "Is Morris out roaming again?"

"He's gone forever this time," Jenny replied. "Two weeks since he left. I'm all alone now."

"He'll be back," I encouraged her. "Besides, you still have your sister in Texas."

Jenny's face saddened further. "No, I don't. She died last month."

Jenny's sister had been her sole surviving relative. *How must she feel with no family members left?* I thought.

My friend's grief swept over me that day. Then, other concerns pushed the news into my do-something-about-it-later cubby hole.

Later that week, a supermarket display of blooming plants caught my attention. *I didn't know about Jenny's loss earlier, but maybe she needs consolation even more now*, I thought. *I'll buy her a plant.*

As I walked up her steps carrying the flowers, Jenny opened the door.

"I'm sorry your sister died," I blurted out, handing her the gift.

Jenny buried her face in the flowers and wept.

The next morning, Jenny was waiting outside her house as I walked by.

"Nobody else cared," she said. "I told everybody on my street. Nobody even said 'I'm sorry.' They said, 'Everybody loses loved ones.' But she was all I had, except for Morris. Only you cared."

I realized how close I had come to joining the others. If the market had featured some other item, I would have forgotten, too.

As I continued on my walk, I prayed, "Walk with me, Lord. Let me see my neighbors as You see them—hurting, lonely, in need. Help me make a difference where I live."

In case you're wondering, Morris returned triumphantly the following week.

Father, give me a caring heart. Teach me compassion. Lend me Your gift of healing. Amen.

Darlene Hoffa is the author of three books. She serves on the advisory board of the Orange County Writers Fellowship and is a free-lance editor. In addition, she critiques the work of other writers. Darlene is married and has three grown children. She enjoys hiking, traveling, and reading. The Hoffas reside in Brea, California.

A Wise Investment

Judy Hyndman

*Teach us to number our days and
recognize how few they are; help us to
spend them as we should.* Psalm 90:12, *TLB*

Dad called the first summer family
meeting to order. Paper and pencils shuffled as each
member wrote his or her list of top summer hits, ways to
spend our tax refund.

Sean, our four-year-old ocean lover, pretended with
his list. "Anyone who wants to go to Pismo Beach, put up
your hand."

"Aye," we all responded.

Mount Hermon Family Camp? San Diego? The annual
church campout? Disneyland?

"An overnight trail ride!" Gwyneth, twelve and keen
on horses, beamed.

Her father's eyes rolled in silent protest. "How about
lots of rest—anywhere?"

Beachfront hotel? County Fair? Cousins Camp?

Theater-fest?

"Wait! How about our remodeling project?" I asked. "I thought we were going to spend some on the house? We could paint and paper and..."

Seeing the looks on their faces, I stopped. What would our children remember when they grew up? The summer of the newly painted walls, or the adventurous father-daughter trail ride? The new doors, or the sumptuous breakfast of sizzling eggs, bacon and shallots, smothered in tortillas, cooked over an open fire? The new wall unit, or the railroad trip to renew friendships? The new carpet, or a Christian camp experience that could help our pre-teen grasp a vision for her future? The new wallpaper, or the church campout where young and old believers build bonds over roasted marshmallows and spirit-filled song?

King David made some mistakes in parenting, yet in Psalm 90 he wisely exhorted us to get our priorities right—to number our days. Our choices reveal much to our children—we invest in what we consider important.

Mentally, I made a new list: *Build a bank of memories to draw on later in life, to comfort, or reinforce a moral decision. Snatch time away from peer pressures and routines to instill God's precepts before the children leave the nest. Create an atmosphere where confidences are revealed and trust is established.* This is numbering our days.

Long, hot afternoons of swimming and hanging out blended into warm evenings of Ping-Pong and root beer floats. We "spent our days as we should." We did curtain the upstairs, but we also invested in a few top summer hits. Years from now, our children will draw from this season of memory-building and say, "And the best part of the summer was..."

Father, give me the wisdom to choose the more important

things in the short time we have to raise Your children.
Amen.

Judy Hyndman has had several articles and devotions published and has a teaching credential in English literature. She enjoys Bible study, classical music, beach walking, photojournaling, and planning activities for family and friends. Judy and her husband have two children and make their home in Los Olivos, California.

A Time to Cry, A Time to Comfort

Carrie Gage Jackson

*Be merciful to me, O Lord, for I am in
distress; my eyes grow weak with sorrow,
my soul and my body with grief.*
Psalm 31:9, *NIV*

Our first baby died just seventy-
seven days after he was born. The grief my husband and
I experienced can only be understood by those who
have also lost a child.

Dustin was born three months prematurely and spent
his entire life in the neonatal unit of a hospital two
hundred miles from our home. During the time he was
fighting for his life, my husband and I were closer to God
than we had ever been. We spent many hours praying by
our baby's bedside and witnessed the answers to many
of those prayers as he struggled to survive.

Then Dustin died, and when we went home empty-
handed, we stopped praying. It seemed like a waste of
time. I questioned why this had been God's will. I felt
forsaken, and I became bitter.

We received many cards, letters, and poems of
comfort, which later became an important part of our
special memories of Dustin, although at the time they did

little to relieve my distress. My grief wouldn't allow anything to touch my heart.

Months later, I reread each one and I was truly touched. This time, the messages helped me realize that God had never left me. Even when I turned my back, He was there, quietly giving me strength to survive my grief.

Finally, my heart allowed the words of a verse to speak to me: "What a wonderful God we have...who so wonderfully comforts and strengthens us in our hardships and trials. And why does he do this? So that when others are troubled, needing our sympathy and encouragement, we can pass on to them this same help and comfort God has given us" (2 Corinthians 1:3-4, *TLB*).

About a year and a half after Dustin died, a woman I barely knew lost her three-year-old to cancer. It touched me in a way I had never known before, and I felt a need to reach out to her. I sat down and wrote a letter beginning with, "Debbie, if you don't feel like reading this now, put it away for a while until you do." Then I poured out my feelings for the loss she had suffered. I expressed my hope that someday she would find comfort in my words.

Since that time, there have been other opportunities to reach out to women who have experienced similar sorrow. While each one is a painful reminder of my own grief, it is also a reminder of the comfort I received.

Thank You, Lord, for giving strength in my sorrow and for teaching me to use my grief to help others. Amen.

Carrie Gage Jackson, besides writing, enjoys reading, biking, mothering, and working with the Awana group at her church. Carrie and her husband, Kenny, have one daughter and make their home in Yuma, Arizona.

Parmesan Cheese and Bacon

Sandie Jarvis

*A father of the fatherless, and a judge of the
widows, is God in his holy habitation.*
Psalms 68:5, *KJV*

Spaghetti sauce was on sale that day and I proudly served up a yummy supper to my family of three children, whom I was raising alone and working full time to support.

"I sure wish we had some Parmesan cheese to put on this," my son said. I understandingly answered something about the last time I priced that item; we exchanged knowing glances and finished our dinner, which was finer than eighty percent of the world ever ate. Small matter indeed that it was without garnish, I thought, while cleaning the kitchen and putting away the borrowed blender I needed to return soon.

The next morning my daughter wanted eggs, bacon, and toast for breakfast. I fixed eggs and toast. Sometimes I get discouraged. The pressures mount, the paycheck never quite lasts until the next one, and there's never anything left to buy extras like bacon.

I often lift my eyes and remind God He has promised to be a father to the fatherless. To me, that means He takes extra special care of my family.

And that is the only explanation for the boxes.

"Would you like some boxes of things I don't want to take when I move?" asked a casual acquaintance at work. "There might be something in them you could use."

There was plenty in them that we could use! "It's like Christmas came early this year," commented my daughter, as she laced up her new shoes. I put the new yellow bowl set in our brown and yellow kitchen. The little box of silverware just happened to be the same as my set.

There was a cake dish to replace the one I had lost. Crisp new sheets, still in unopened packages, would replace the worn ones on our beds. There was even a blender so I could return the borrowed one. And, oh yes, there was bacon—and Parmesan cheese.

Thank You, Lord, for showing me once again that I can completely trust You to keep Your promises, and that I don't have to carry all the responsibility for my children by myself. Amen.

Sandie Jarvis has published several articles. Besides writing, she enjoys music, gardening, canning foods, and working with Good News (Bible) Club. Sandie has three grown children and resides in Wenatchee, Washington.

Seasons of Sorrow

Barbara Lee Johnson

Weeping may endure for a night, but joy cometh in the morning. Psalm 30:5, *KJV*

Often, it is difficult for me to understand that sorrow is not something to be possessed, but rather a gift that is lent for a period of time. The Apostle Peter says sorrow is only for a season and is permitted by God for our faith to grow (1 Peter 1:6-7). In fact, Peter calls it the trial of our faith.

Nothing stretches faith like the fires of sorrow and grief. That must be why the Apostle Paul wrote these words to the Corinthian Christians: "For our light affliction, which is but for a moment, worketh for us a far more exceeding and eternal weight of glory" (2 Corinthians 4:17). He knew that affliction—and surely sorrow and grief are afflictions—is a working process that brings forth positive results.

Somehow I never looked at sorrow as temporary until the other morning. Suddenly, I realized that sorrow is not something we are to possess, but rather a thing we are to go through to get to the other side. As the sorrow goes on and becomes harder to bear, the things that are seen try to take us away from the things that are not seen. But sorrow is not eternal, it is temporal. The

Scriptures teach us that we are not to look at sorrow, but to look at what lies beyond the sorrow. And that is joy!

When King David wrote Psalm 30, he knew and understood the weeping, but he had also tasted the joy. Surely, our heavenly Father's gift to us is eternal joy. Although sorrow is a temporary thing, joy is not. It is eternal.

I want to use the sorrows in my life to draw me nearer to the heart of God. I want to accept the sorrows as a sacred trust lent to me by a Father who loves me and desires only what is best for my life. I may endure crying for a night, but I'm so thankful His Word promises that joy comes in the morning.

O Father, on that joyful morning when You shall wipe away all tears and sorrow, when I shall understand the unexplained, I will thank and praise You for the seasons of sorrow that opened my eyes to the exquisite tenderness of Your divine love. Amen.

Barbara Lee Johnson is the author of three books, including *Count It All Joy.* She is a conference speaker and leads seminars across the country. Barbara enjoys golf and tennis. She and her husband, Don, have two grown sons and make their home in Orlando, Florida.

A Witness

Carolyn Johnson

*I said, "I will watch my ways and keep my
tongue from sin; I will put a muzzle on
my mouth."* Psalm 39:1, *NIV*

Dust billowed around the wheels of
our motorhome, as Harry backed into our assigned space
in the rustic campground. At six o'clock in the evening,
the Arizona sun still beat relentlessly upon our temporary
home. It had been a long day of driving, and we were
both tired and hungry.

"Not a tree in sight," I grumbled. "Is this the best you
could do?"

"Look around. The campground is full." Harry's
answer was curt.

I jumped down from the cab to inspect the facilities.
"Oh, this is great," I said, sarcasm coating my words.
"There's not even a table here! We should have stopped
at the last place, like I suggested."

Harry uncoiled the electric cord from its storage
compartment and plugged it into the receptacle. "Why
don't you put the coffee on, and then we'll go for a swim
and cool off."

"And who's going to be getting dinner while I'm in
the pool? You may remember that's why I wanted to stop
earlier. If you'd only listen..."

166

The people in the neighboring campsite looked up as my voice got louder. I walked to the back of our rig to avoid their curious stares. I knew how I sounded, and I was ashamed.

As I stood there trying to compose myself, my eyes fell upon the fish. It's the symbol of our Christianity, prominently displayed above the back bumper of our motorhome. We'd put it there to proclaim our faith, to tell the world that we choose to follow Christ—even as we follow the highways and byways across our beautiful country. But how could others hear the song in my heart when I smothered it with words of resentment and self-pity?

Harry was hooking up the water hose when I walked back and put my arm around him. He turned in surprise, then smiled. "Sorry I'm such a crab, honey," I said. "I do need to cool off. Let's get our suits on. We can have fried-egg sandwiches for dinner."

Lord, help me to be an instrument of Your peace, to speak words of love instead of bitterness. Help me remember that I am Your witness in this world. Amen.

Carolyn Johnson is the author of several articles and the recently released book *How To Blend a Family*. She enjoys Bible study, church activities, and traveling. She and her husband, Harry, have a blended family of nine adult children. The Johnsons reside in Solvang, California.

Season of Humility

Jan Johnson

*He guides the humble in what is right and
teaches them his way.* Psalm 25:9, *NIV*

"Sometimes she drives the pretty
blue Honda; other times she has that old wreck," giggled
Erin, one of my lively eighth-grade students.

I swallowed hard, rounded the corner, and smiled at
Erin.

She was right. The car I drove was embarrassing. It
was twenty-five years old and looked even older. We
bought it from a "little old lady" who had gently
sideswiped both sides of the car on her bright yellow
house. The rear of the car sported irregular stripes of
blue and aqua from a chest she had hit in her garage.
The rim of the right headlight was crinkled. And the
stuffing from the seats snowflaked onto my crisp
teaching suits.

Why did we buy it? My husband, Greg, was out of
work; it was the best we could afford at the time. And
the car ran well, even if it wasn't glamorous.

I often told Greg how dependable I thought the car
was. Yet on weekends I'd try to run errands first so I
could use his car instead.

I tried to keep this ragged old car from strangling my

self-esteem. At first, I sneaked out to the church parking lot so friends wouldn't see me get into it. Gradually, I developed quips to keep people's negative comments at bay. Instead of apologizing for it, I dismissed the gazes of my children's friends with, "Isn't this car great? It's an antique!"

Driving that car forced me to reject the idea that a woman is what she drives, where she lives, and how she dresses. I learned to giggle when church members stared at me as I exited the parking lot. Then I'd look at myself in the rearview mirror and chortle, "God's already seen me in this car and He thinks I'm terrific."

Eventually we bought a better, not-so-used car and gave the old car away. I look back and feel thankful that I drove it. There was at least one time in my life when I cast the worldly trappings aside and knew who I was in God's eyes.

Thank You, Lord, for the humiliations I must go through that teach me that You alone are my source of importance and strength. Amen.

Jan Johnson has published numerous articles, book reviews, and devotions. She is currently the book review columnist for *Today's Christian Woman.* Jan enjoys reading and she works with Christian support groups for women with eating disorders and adult children of alcoholics. She and her husband, Greg, have two children and make their home in Inglewood, California.

Wait for
the Lord

Sharon K. Johnson

*I wait for the Lord, my soul waits, and in his
word I put my hope.* Psalm 130:5, *NIV*

Recently, while walking along an
isolated beach, I cried out to God for His guidance and
assurance about a particular area of my life. I pleaded,
"Speak to me, Lord, Your servant listens."

Then I heard the still small voice that stirs within the
heart, "Sharon, wait! I have something for you, but you
must wait for the blessing. Be obedient; walk closely
with Me. Don't always try to run ahead of Me."

I pondered as I walked, and soon stopped to watch a
great blue heron catch a fish. As I stood silently and
waited, my eye caught movement far down the beach.
Several hundred yards ahead, a doe and a young fawn
leaped from the bank onto the sand. I'd walked this
beach for four summers, seeing tracks and hoping to see
deer.

I started to quietly follow them, but decided to sit
down instead. The deer hadn't seen me. They started
coming my way. I crouched low.

Suddenly they ran towards me, stopping scarcely a
hundred feet away. They saw me. I continued to sit
quietly, hardly breathing. To my amazement, they

walked stealthily toward me. Cautious, ears twitching, black eyes wide with curiosity, they approached—50 feet, 25 feet, 15 feet.

"Lord," I prayed, "I don't believe this is happening. For years I've watched for one deer, and today two are investigating me. Is this a sign from You? Are You telling me if I wait patiently, You will bless me for my obedience?" I felt God's confirming presence.

After scrutinizing me for several moments, the deer turned and bounded off down the beach. I sat in awe of what God had allowed to happen.

I thought of all the times I've tried to run ahead of Him, trying to accomplish everything in my own wisdom and strength. God used this experience to show me just how much I need to go to Him in prayer, wait for His guidance, and depend upon His Word.

Thank You, Lord, for showing me I don't need to have all the answers right now. Please help me trust You more. I need to be still and wait for You, and put my hope in Your Word. Amen.

Sharon K. Johnson has had numerous articles published. She enjoys photography, art, hiking, backpacking, cross-country skiing, working with Junior High groups, and leading Bible studies. Sharon and her husband, Bob, have four children and make their home in Issaquah, Washington.

Step by Step

Shirley Joiner

*Thy word is a lamp [candle] unto my
feet, and a light unto my path.*
Psalm 119:105, *KJV*

Our family wanted to find a winter
sport that we could all enjoy and decided to try snow
skiing. So, when Ethan's fifth-grade class took ski lessons
at Hemlock Mountain, I volunteered to chauffeur. *Here is
an excellent opportunity to join the other beginners and
learn a new sport*, I thought.

Feeling terribly awkward strapped into stiff ski boots,
I tried not to appear clumsy as I followed the instructor
to the bunny hill.

Learning to ski was a thrilling experience. I
discovered I had the courage to conquer the fear of
dangling in a chair lift, standing on the edge of a scary
incline of moguls, being too cold, and breaking bones.

Skiing Big White in British Columbia last February
taught me something more, however. The mountain was
enshrouded in dense fog when we reached the top, and
visibility was not more than a meter. The run was one I
had not skied before. It didn't intimidate me though,
because I couldn't see much beyond the tips of my skis.
Even a beginner can ski three feet without fear. Steadily, I
made my way down without a fall.

The next day the fog lifted. When I saw the mountain slope clearly, I panicked. "I can't do it!" I exclaimed to my husband. "Look how steep it is!"

"You did it yesterday, didn't you?" he replied.

"Yes, but yesterday I couldn't see how hard it was."

"Come on, let's go," he said, and down he went. Cautiously, I started the decline, diagonally cutting across the precipitous slope. Just then it occurred to me how in life God allows me to see just enough of the path ahead. If allowed to see too far in advance, I might panic and say, "I can't do it."

God's Word is a candle (not a floodlight) to my feet. I know I can do whatever He calls me to do—one step at a time.

Father, order my steps aright. Thank You for enough light, grace, and strength for each step of the way. Amen.

Shirley Joiner, besides writing, enjoys interior decorating, tennis, skiing, and Israeli folk dancing. She is a fashion/color consultant and personal development instructor. Shirley and her husband, Dennis, have one son and reside in Abbotsford, British Columbia.

Out of Deep Waters

Debbie Kalmbach

*He reached down from on high and took
hold of me; he drew me out of deep waters.
He rescued me from my powerful enemy,
from my foes, who were too strong for me.*
Psalm 18:16-17, *NIV*

In an instant, our rafting trip down
the Snoqualmie River turned into a nightmare, as the
swift run-off current caught our raft and propelled it
toward a downed tree.

"We're going to hit!" my husband cried. We paddled
frantically to avoid the collision. When I heard the
explosion of bursting vinyl, I knew we were in trouble.
Air hissed from the raft. We plunged into the icy water.
The force of the current crushed us against a limb.

"I can't breathe," Randy gasped. The panic in his
voice terrified me. He struggled to free himself and
finally was able to push away from the log. I watched as
the river swept him downstream. He grabbed a branch
and hung on, then clawed his way onto the trunk.

I dug my fingernails into the limb and ached from the
freezing water. "I can't hang on much longer."

"You'll have to let go, Deb. You'll only be underwater

for a few seconds; I'll catch you on the other side." His steady, confident tone calmed me.

With childlike faith, I obeyed. Raging water tumbled over me. My strength was no match for the powerful current. Just as he had promised, my husband grabbed hold of me and pulled me out. We both wept as he held me in his arms—safe at last.

God has reached down many times and rescued me from dangerous situations. Before I accepted Him as Savior, I was on a collision course. I stubbornly clung to my ways. The harder I tried, the more weary and frustrated I became. It wasn't until I let go of my will and surrendered to God's, that I was freed. He drew me out of confusion and turmoil and placed me on solid ground.

Thank You, dear Lord, not only for sparing our lives that spring morning, but for saving me spiritually. You released me from the clutches of sin, a foe much too powerful for me. I am safe in Your arms always. Amen.

Debbie Kalmbach has written several articles. She enjoys reading, swimming, and cross-stitch. She ministers in a support group for families and friends of those addicted to alcohol and drugs. Debbie and her husband, Randy, have two sons and reside in Auburn, Washington.

Instant Potatoes

Pat Kampenga

*I would have despaired unless I had
believed that I would see the goodness of the
Lord in the land of the living. Wait for the
Lord; be strong, and let your heart take
courage; Yes, wait for the Lord.*
Psalm 27:13-14, *NASB*

He lay there, ashen in color. Straining with each breath, he was just a shell of the man he had once been.

"I want to die," he said.

"Are you ready?" she asked.

"Yes," came the faint reply.

A few moments later, she saw his mouth moving as if he were speaking, but no sound came from his lips.

"What are you saying?" she asked.

"I'm asking forgiveness," was the answer.

I wasn't with my father-in-law when he uttered those words the day before his death; they were related to me by my sister-in-law. But I received them with the same sense of praise and thanksgiving I would have felt had I heard them myself, for I had been praying for him for twelve years.

Because I had prayed so often about this and other

matters without seeing immediate results, I had come to think I'd have to wait till heaven to know how my prayers for my father-in-law would be answered. I guess because I have instant coffee, instant potatoes—even instant television replay—I assumed I'd have instant answers to my prayers. And many times, because I didn't see immediate results, I thought God had forgotten about my needs and requests.

But He has promised that He answers while I am yet asking, and although I came across this verse many years ago while praying about another matter, the Lord used my father-in-law to remind me that I will see God's goodness in the land of the living.

Lord, help me to be patient for Your answers, knowing that You will, indeed, answer. Amen.

Pat Kampenga has written Bible stories for children. She is a lecturer and Bible study leader. Pat is married and is the mother of three children. The Kampengas make their home in Burbank, California.

Help, I'm Dyeing

Nancy Kennedy

*Blessed is he whose transgressions are
forgiven, whose sins are covered. Blessed is
the man whose sin the Lord does not count
against him and in whose spirit is no deceit.*
Psalm 32:1-2, *NIV*

It all began when I poured bleach
into the washing machine and it splashed onto the sleeve
of my new blue shirt, making a white spot.

"No problem—I can dye it," I reassured myself.

I sat on the edge of my bathtub. As it filled with hot
water, I dumped in the package of royal blue fabric dye,
swishing it around with a wooden spoon. When I put my
shirt into the dye-water, the spoon fell in too. I reached
in to get it, causing my skin to turn blue up to my elbow.
Lifting the now-blue spoon out, I lost my balance and
accidentally flung it across the room. In the process, I
splattered the pink shorts and aqua T-shirt I was wearing,
the white towels hanging on the towel bar, the wall
behind them, and the peach bath rug.

Not one to be easily discouraged, I took off my shorts
and T-shirt and tossed them in the tub, along with the
towels and the rug. "I might as well dye them all," I
thought to myself.

After ten minutes, I drained the water and stared at the royal blue stain covering the entire once-white bathtub.

"No problem—I can bleach it later."

Then I rinsed out the rug, towels, shorts, and two shirts. To my dismay, I discovered—after all that trouble—the dye hadn't even covered the bleached spot on my shirt, and I had ruined everything else in the process. In taking matters into my own hands, I had only succeeded in making a mess.

Second Samuel 11 tells the story of King David, who committed adultery with Bathsheba. He tried to cover up the resulting pregnancy by ordering the murder of Uriah, Bathsheba's husband, thereby causing bitter anguish for everyone involved. It wasn't until David confessed his sin to God and admitted, "Against you, you only, have I sinned and done what is evil in your sight" (Psalm 51:4), that David's sin could be covered.

What a mess we make whenever we take matters into our own hands instead of bringing them to the Lord.

Dear Lord, my efforts to cover my sin cannot remove it—only Your shed blood can do that. Thank You that Your forgiveness and cleansing are available to me whenever I ask for them. Amen.

Nancy Kennedy, besides writing, enjoys sewing for her children, quilting, baking, country crafts, and quilt-making. She and her husband, Barry, have two daughters. The Kennedys make their home in Marina, California.

Powerful Providence

Denella Kimura

*He covers the heavens with clouds, he
prepares rain for the earth, he makes grass
grow upon the hills.* Psalm 147:8, *RSV*

Lightning whizzed, cracked, and split
the sky, as invisible giants tore the clouds into rags. The
resulting downpour of rain fed the earth enough water to
make sprinkler systems unnecessary for days. Then the
sun parted the nimbus monoliths and turned the rain into
tinsel. In the west the clouds broke into shards around
the shafted light.

In my rose garden the plants extended rain-dipped
leaves and dew-lined petals to the sundown sparklers.
The moss roses folded prematurely for their evening
siesta, and my youngest son splashed barefoot through
gutter puddles.

I think of last year's drought and thank God for the
rain that changes the foothill grasses from gold to green,
quenches thirsty plants, fills the reservoirs and streams,
and seeps deep to the roots of ancient oaks. And, yes, I
even thank Him for puddles just for little boys to splash
through.

It isn't natural for me to be thankful for storms. I think
of the many times I've complained of the rain: There

were the inconveniences of power outages at dinnertime, snarled traffic on slippery freeways, garage doors
that had to be opened manually instead of automatically,
and activities restricted because of lightning. Yet God
gave us the grace to endure the problems, while thrilling
us with the glory of His power.

As a family, we recently went through a great
spiritual storm when my husband had difficulties with his
job. Soon after accepting a new position, we were
transferred to the area where we now live. I rebelled at
the changes and uprooting of my life and all the family
adjustments required by such a move. Yet through it all
we saw God's hand at work, relieving the stresses caused
by the turmoil of relocating a family. I praise Him for His
powerful presence which took us through the tempest.

*Lord, when I experience spiritual storms, help me look for
the display of Your power and thank You for the ultimate
good You alone can bring. Amen.*

Denella Kimura has authored several articles and poems. In
addition, she does poetry readings and seminars for women and
children. She enjoys sketching, watercolor painting, singing,
drama, and gardening. Denella and her husband, Tom, have
three sons and reside in Roseville, California.

What Color Is Discontent?

Carla Anne Kirk

Cleanse me with hyssop, and I will be clean;
wash me, and I will be whiter than snow.
Psalm 51:7, *NIV*

On a scale of one to ten, my
appearance was a minus five that day. I had no intention
of going out; the snow was five inches deep on the drive
and walkway and I was already three days into a room
renovation that had been put off far too long. How I
looked seemed of little importance.

With great care, I rolled the pale pink paint over the
walls, determined to finish the project by evening. The
sudden knock at my door irritated me, and, as I wiped
my paint-smeared hands across my shirttails, I glared at
the teenage boy standing there. "Yes?"

"May I walk your shovel?" he muttered.

Perhaps I had heard him wrong; perhaps three days
of paint fumes had befuddled my mind. "What?"

"May I walk your shovel?"

Suppressing my laughter, I said, "My husband always
shovels our walk. Thank you. No."

As the boy trudged sadly away through the snow, his look perplexed, I wondered when he would realize his blunder. I also wondered about the cause of the odd expression on his face. The answer to that dilemma, however, dawned on me as I neared the hall mirror.

"What an impression I've made," I grumbled, laughing at myself. I looked disheveled after three days of absorption with a project that had cast out all thought of my appearance, just as the past eight years of struggling to renovate our Victorian dream house had played similar havoc with my heart.

I was unlovely, bespattered with poor attitudes, self-pity, regret, and defeat—all of which asked of God, "Why did You do this to me? Why do I have to contend with a leaky roof, an antiquated heating system, mold, cracked walls, and rain-scarred ceilings? Why!!!?" And the discontent had grown into a life-style; it had settled deep into my heart, until the root of bitterness had grown like a cancer to mar every phase of my life.

The day the boy came to clean the walk became a day of reckoning for me. His confused reaction helped me to know my outward appearance had been ignored far too long, just as my response to him showed me the condition of my innermost being.

The Holy Spirit spoke a message that had not become garbled at my heart's door. No, this message was clear: "God is not pleased."

With this understanding came an inkling of what life could be like, if only I would submit to God. Since peace of mind had long escaped me, I began to realize that peace with God was the treasure that could end years of rebellion and wipe clean a heart in disarray.

God, when You look on my heart and see it marred with sin from discontent, You are not confused, nor unprepared. When all within me is stained and disheveled, Your purification is complete, leaving no unsightly speck of wrong. Truly, the cleansing of my heart has proved more precious than silver. Amen.

Carla Anne Kirk has been writing since junior high school and is currently writing a novel. She is the director of a sacred dance choir and ministers with two dance troupes. Carla and her husband have three sons and make their home in Wilmington, Delaware.

He Keeps
Me Close

Berit Kjos

The Lord is your keeper. Psalm 121:5, *NASB*

"Prone to wander, Lord, I know it..."
Can you identify with the words of this old hymn? I
can. Some days my mind wanders; it doesn't remain
focused on my King. Some days my heart wanders; I am
restless and search for all sorts of satisfactions outside His
kingdom. I find it hard to settle down with my Bible; and
though my heart wants to sing only songs of the King, I
sing the world's songs, which stir longings not from Him.
I know that I love Him most of all, but I wonder if I'm
drifting away.

Then I remember that Jesus has promised to keep
me. I am safe; He will never let me go. Quietly, He
confirms my thoughts with His Word: "He will not allow
your foot to slip; He who keeps you will not slumber"
(Psalm 121:3).

"Trust me," He whispers, "for I will hold you by the
hand and watch over you."

I may sleep, but my Keeper remains awake and alert.
And, again and again, He awakens my heart to love Him
more, for He sees the longing of my heart. He allows me
to pass through storms and fires that force me to rely on
Him, not on myself. But as He trains me to be His Bride,

He whispers His promise, "I will protect you from all evil; I will keep your soul. I will guard each step you take from this time forth and forever."

Though my thoughts wander, I remain His precious child. I belong to Him; He has full custody over me, and nothing can separate me from His love! Again and again, He assures me, "I will never fail you nor forsake you" (Hebrews 13:5, *RSV*).

I cannot understand such love, but I receive it with all my heart. There is no place more wonderful than in the loving hands of my Keeper.

Precious Lord, thank You for drawing me close and hiding me in Yourself. Thank You for guarding me even as You transform me into Your likeness. In You I am content. Amen.

Berit Kjos has authored many Bible studies as well as two books. Since completing *Your Child and the New Age*, she has enjoyed helping parents train children to resist spiritual deception. Berit and her husband, Andy, have three sons and live in Los Altos, California.

My Dwelling Place

Eleanore Klassen

*Lord, you have been our dwelling place
throughout all generations.* Psalm 90:1, *NIV*

It had been a busy fall. We had moved from our first home to a new area and new house we had built. After the first hectic weeks of cleaning and painting and trying to locate everything we had packed, we finally felt settled in.

Now I was ready to look for friendly faces. Coming from a small community, I was accustomed to close ties with neighbors and church members. I was quite confident I would have no trouble making friends and was sure my outgoing personality would help me quickly establish relationships.

In church that Sunday morning, I glanced around at all the strangers. How could I know if they were newcomers like myself or charter members who might take offense if I seemed pushy? I no longer felt confident. This eight-hundred-member church was so different from my small community church of eighty members, where all seemed like family. Could I really feel at home here?

During the following week, I looked out of my just-cleaned windows at rows of shiny new houses. Vacant windows stared back at me, mirroring the deserted street.

"Does anyone live there?" I mused to myself. "Does anyone have time for a cup of tea?" The phone never rang; the doorbell never chimed.

Loneliness settled over me like a thick fog. After moping for a while and shedding a few tears, I finally realized that God had a promise for this situation. I had only changed location geographically; He was still my "dwelling place." It did not matter where I lived—He was there!

Gradually, I began to recognize people in the congregation on Sunday mornings, and I distinctly remember the day I sat in my pew and said to myself, "This is my church!"

By early December, I had regained my courage and knocked at all of those shiny new doors to invite my neighbors to an open house. I was thankful that God was, and is, my dwelling place. Now I could share my new house with my new friends and introduce them to the One who made it home for me.

Father, I thank You for the assurance of Your presence, wherever I live. You are my dwelling place; this gives me great security. Amen.

Eleanore Klassen is co-author of one book and author of several articles. Besides writing and reading, she enjoys growing roses, sewing, crafts, walking, and singing. She heads up the women's ministry and prayer ministry at her church. Eleanore and her husband, Arthur, have three grown children and reside in Abbotsford, British Columbia.

Hope

Louise Hannah Kohr

*Be of good courage, and he shall strengthen
your heart, all ye that hope in the Lord.*
Psalm 31:24, *KJV*

When I was told Ty Moffatt had
died, my heart was like a stone in my breast. His wife,
Elizabeth, and I were fast friends. I would have to go to
her. How I dreaded it.

Elizabeth and Ty had been so devoted. They were
always at church together. In the few instances where
one could nót be there, the other remained at home.
Though there were spare hymnals, they sang from one,
as though they sang better together.

They always had a fine garden. They specialized in
prize-winning roses. When Ty worked outside, Elizabeth,
in her battered old garden hat, worked alongside him.
When she washed dishes, he dried them.

Now Ty was gone. What would Elizabeth do without
him? He always said that no one could rub a tired back
like Liz could. And she said that he ate burned toast like
he hankered for it.

I walked in without knocking. She was in the little
parlor, with its cross-stitched motto "God Bless Our
Home" over the hewn-log fireplace, in her favorite
rocker, reading her Bible.

The look on her face will remain in my memory forever. It was more a look of wonder than of sorrow. *The men of Emmaus must have looked so as they hurried to tell the disciples they had seen Jesus*, I thought.

"Elizabeth!" I fell on my knees before her.

"God was here last night," she said serenely. "He took Ty with Him." No tears, just a sort of elation as though heaven were as near as the other room.

"He will be coming back for me. I've only to tend the roses 'til He comes."

Lord Jesus, help me to know the meaning of hope that only You can give. I want to treasure it in my heart of hearts. Amen.

Louise Hannah Kohr is the author of numerous devotions, articles, and stories. Besides writing, she enjoys reading and spending time in her flower beds. Louise is married and, with her husband, makes her home in Olympia, Washington.

Sweet Suffering

Penny S. Kwiat

*Surely when the mighty waters rise, they
will not reach him [me]. You are my hiding
place; you will protect me from trouble and
surround me with the songs of deliverance.*
Psalm 32:6-7, *NIV*

Waking up at 4:30 A.M. was never
my idea of a good time. Managing to roll out of bed, I
made my way to the bathroom to prepare myself for a
six-hour flight to be with my sick and nearly dying
mother. It was a day of expectancy and dread.

I pondered the words of David in Psalm 32. Even
though my stomach was in knots, God's Word was such
a comfort. *Yes, the mighty waters rise, but they will not
reach me! Oh, God, You are my hiding place!*

I have grown since that telephone call from my
father, asking if I could come and be with Mother at this
difficult time. God enabled me to minister to my parents
in ways they had ministered to me when I was growing
up. It was an honor and rare privilege to pray with my
mom each day and do the everyday tasks about the
house for her.

Since those weeks of obedience, when I left my three
children and dear husband to go across the country and

minister to my parents, God has blessed our family with both sets of parents moving in with us. We enjoy their sweet company and their strength in Jesus. God has truly given us "songs of deliverance!"

Mother's cancer is ever-present, but the work God has done in the lives of each of our family members, as we've ministered to Mother, is a gift from Him—a tool used to bring us closer to Him—and each other.

Psalm 32:10 tells us, "Many are the woes of the wicked, but the Lord's unfailing love surrounds the man who trusts in him." Some days, I feel as if the mighty waters are about to overtake me. And when I do, I take heart, for my God is mighty, yet gentle, and He will instruct me and teach me in the way I should go (verse 8).

Our family would all agree, that in the midst of dealing with such a devastating and crippling disease as cancer, we have a song in our hearts. We're blessed today because we know that He will surround us with songs of deliverance.

Precious Heavenly Father, thank You for allowing me the privilege of ministering to my parents as they so lovingly ministered to me while I was growing up. Thank You, too, for being there when I need You to give me courage and strength when the mighty waters of life arise. Amen.

Penny S. Kwiat is active in her church, playing the piano, teaching Sunday School and discipleship training, directing a women's group, and leading a kids' night. She and her husband, Chester, have three children and reside in Duvall, Washington.

The Exalted Housewife

Carrie Ladrido

*O Lord, truly I am Your servant; I am Your
servant, the son of Your maidservant. You
have loosed my bonds, I will offer to You
the sacrifice of thanksgiving.*
Psalm 116:16-17, *NKJV*

I knew the inevitable question was
coming. My teeth clenched with anticipation.

"You quit your nursing job to do what?" My friend's
astounded face was almost a taunt.

"To stay home and be a mom and homemaker," I
intoned.

"You mean a servant!" she laughed. I was used to this
reaction from former workmates, but the derision never
quite lost its sting.

"You threw away all that schooling, training, and a
decent wage, just to stay home? Your husband could
have hired a slave to do the housework!" The comments
are always the same.

In today's world, more and more homemakers join
the work force. Full-time wives and mothers who stay at
home often feel as though they're either members of a
dying breed or are lacking mentally. Yet being a
homemaker is a demanding job. Just ask any woman

whose daily tasks include: five loads of laundry, catering three meals, refereeing fourteen fights, and shuttling about a station wagon load of would-be dancers, baseball stars, and piano players. Not to mention, tending to skinned knees, broken toys, and wounded egos!

Homemakers shouldn't have to hide or gloss over their profession. God created women as helpmates to men; we hold a valued place in the balance of God's world.

Perhaps in the world's eyes I am a slave. But I'm an emancipated servant! Jesus Christ loosed me, and, out of a thankful heart, I serve my family. To do my best as a housewife and mother is to be my best for the Lord.

Dirty footprints mar my freshly shampooed carpets. "What's it all for?" I throw up my hands and scrub mud. But the Lord sees the diligence applied to my tasks, and, if it pleases Him, that is my sacrifice of thanksgiving.

I may not enjoy the benefits of dual incomes, but, as a maidservant of the Lord, my reward comes in raising my children and in a stack of clean, folded laundry and in freshly baked chocolate chip cookies. In all these ways I serve God.

Lord, often the world sees my job as a thankless servant's task. Help me to see my job as You see it—valued. You appointed me, Lord. Let me please You. Amen.

Carrie Ladrido teaches her church teen Bible study. Besides writing, she enjoys managing the family's mini-farm. Carrie and her husband, Rick, have two sons and make their home in Graham, Washington.

My
Fulfilled Nest

Kathleen R. Lewis

*I remember the days of long ago; I meditate
on all your works and consider what your
hands have done.* Psalm 143:5, *NIV*

A well-meaning friend spied my
husband and me walking into church, not long after we
had taken our youngest daughter off to college.

"Hey, you two," he said with a wink, "how's your
empty nest?"

I wanted to say, "Empty!" Instead, I bubbled on for a
moment or two about the obvious fringe benefits of
privacy and fewer responsibilities.

My adjustment was only beginning. With no school
schedule to follow for the first time in twenty-six years, I
felt strangely caught in an endless summer. Every day felt
like a weekend.

One side of the house lay silent: neither towels,
bedding, nor clothes moved. It occurred to me that my
husband and I were living in one section of a very
familiar model home. And although there were, indeed,
many wonderful advantages to being a couple again, my
heart was breaking.

I wanted my children back, not grown-up, but small
again. I wanted them back in their highchairs or lying on

the floor doing their homework while watching the Brady Bunch. I wanted a carload of noisy kids on their way home from school.

Previously, my entire life was centered around full-time mothering. Now, I felt like I had been involuntarily retired from the best job in the world, one I had loved completely. Of course, my nostalgia was not rational, but it was part of my necessary journey to acceptance.

With the following months came many ups and downs, but soon a new pattern came into my thinking. I began to be filled with an overwhelming sense of thanksgiving for the privilege of having been given these children. The fact that I had finished this part of my life's work brought with it a tremendous satisfaction that was difficult to describe.

As God has carried me tenderly through this past year, one thing has become clear: God's plan for my life is not to be feared. I can fully trust the One who guides me through this transition. I can rest securely in His comfort and look to the future with hope and excitement.

Now when someone mentions my empty nest, I can say with a smile, "It still feels empty. But the truth is, my nest is fulfilled!" And I thank God once more for allowing me to have the best job in the world.

Lord of all my days, help me to find new ways to serve You, new outlets for my time and energies, and new joy in walking with You. Thank You with my whole heart for Your changeless, matchless love. Amen.

Kathleen R. Lewis, besides writing, enjoys reading, singing, needlepoint, cooking, and being near the beach. She is active in women's ministries and outreach luncheons for her community. Kathleen and her husband have three grown daughters and reside in San Rafael, California.

God Has a Thousand Ways

Vivian M. Loken

*Let them give thanks to the Lord for his
unfailing love...for he satisfies the thirsty
and fills the hungry with good things.*
Psalm 107:8-9, *NIV*

I was walking home from school, my
heart as bruised as the scuffed-up toes of my shoes.
Perhaps partially due to living in a remote area, school to
me was the next thing to paradise. I loved to read and
every day's literary adventures offered new glimpses into
other worlds. My sadness was because I had read every
single book available.

When you're eleven years old and your reasoning
power is limited, the world can look pretty bleak. I
envisioned the rest of my life as an endless corridor with
empty bookshelves on both sides.

Many years have gone by since that day of particular
heartbreak. Now, because I am a writer, there are books
all over the place. I have books on loan from libraries,

and I'm blessed with owning a great many others. My riches include more than one Bible, several dictionaries, and a set of encyclopedias. I don't know how this happened, but I'm sure it testifies to the goodness of God.

Although I no longer suffer from a lack of books, I do have other lacks in my life that cause heartache. One particular need often threatens to drive me to despair, so I bring it, along with fervent praise and thanks, to God's attention daily. As in Psalm 38:9: "All my longings lie open before you, O Lord..."

When I become too preoccupied with misery, letting it rob my attention from everything else, I look around me. Books strewn across the floor, lying open on tables and standing on shelves with mute invitation, remind me that "he satisfies the thirsty and fills the hungry." Stopping to remember how that need has been gratified, I feel hopeful.

It is my nature to keep trying to find a way to overcome any problem, even though I have yielded it to God. The efforts I make help for awhile, but then I reach the end of my resources. Another writer, Esther Guyot, puts it in these words:

God has a thousand ways
Where I can see not one,
When all my means have reached their end,
*Then His have just begun.**

My creative imagination cannot conceive of a way that the emptiness in my life can be filled. Of course, neither did I see that someday I would have enough books to please even me.

O Lord, how I lean on the promise of Your unfailing love that satisfies the thirsty and fills the hungry with good things. Help me to remember to continue giving thanks, as gratitude breeds hope. Amen.

Inspiring Quotations compiled by Albert M. Wells, Jr.

Vivian M. Loken has written numerous poems and articles for publication and has published two books of poetry. She enjoys homemaking, gardening, and photography. She and her husband have one son and have raised two other children. The Lokens reside in Minneapolis, Minnesota.

Trusting God

Catherine Marshall

Commit your way to the Lord—roll and repose [each care of] your load on Him; trust (lean on, rely on and be confident) also in Him, and He will bring it to pass.
Psalm 37:5, *AMP*

There is much in Scripture stressing our need to have faith in God. The above verse takes us a step further. It not only admonishes us to trust, it promises that when we do, God will act in a supernatural way to answer our need. Dwell on that for a moment. We trust, God acts. A mind-blowing premise.

Yet total, all-out trust on our part is not as easy as it first seems. There are periods when God's face is shrouded, when His dealings with us will *appear* as if He does not care, when He seems not to be acting like a true Father. Can we then hang onto the fact of His love and His faithfulness and that He *is* a prayer-answering God?

Can we get to the point Habakkuk reached: "Though the fig tree does not blossom, and there be no fruit on the vines...Yet I will rejoice in the Lord...!" (Habakkuk 3:17-18, *AMP*).

Can we, *at the moment* when His face is hidden,

exult in the God of our salvation? "The Lord God is my strength, my personal bravery and my invincible army" (v.19).

Last Saturday morning [my husband] Len had a chance to demonstrate the principle of trust in a difficult situation. He awoke with a very bad throat condition; could hardly speak. Yet he was supposed to give a talk that morning at a men's prayer breakfast in the local Lutheran church.

Before he left for the church I anointed him with oil, placed my hand on his throat, and asked the Lord to do a healing work in Len for the glory of God.

During the breakfast preceding Len's speech, however, he told me later, his voice got worse and worse until there was little left but a croak. The Lutheran pastor suggested turning the gathering into a discussion group, giving Len the chance to bow out. But no, my husband would at least try.

So Len stood up and uttered a rasping, halting first sentence, literally plunging ahead on faith. Suddenly, he reported afterwards, his voice cleared. From then on, for thirty-odd minutes, the message poured out with no cough, hardly even a clearing of the throat. The Holy Spirit had simply taken over. In the question period afterwards, still no problem with his throat.

But when he returned home, Len's voice was once again a painful whisper.

What fascinated me in this episode is how biblical it is: as the symptoms get worse, the temptation is there to "give up" and not to trust Jesus. We must resist that temptation in the midst of our very real human helplessness, "roll" the entire burden onto His shoulders, as He bade us do, step out and *take the first step* with bare, no-evidence-at-all faith.

And lo, He does take over gloriously, doing what we literally cannot do for ourselves.

Thank You, Lord, for the promise in Your Word that if we

but turn our cares over to You, You will, supernaturally and without reserve, intercede on our behalves. You are a wonderful loving Father who cares about our every need. Amen.

Catherine Marshall, author of twenty-one books including bestsellers like *Christy*, *A Man Called Peter*, *Something More*, and *Beyond Ourselves*, died in 1983. Over the years her books have touched the hearts of millions of readers, both Christian and non-Christians alike. Catherine will long be remembered as one of America's most beloved inspirational writers.

Opening Doors

Joan Martin

*For the Lord watches over all the plans and
paths of godly men.* Psalm 1:6, *TLB*

You'd think I'd have gotten used to
moving around the country by now. I've done it seven
times in the years I've been married. But it's never been
easy for me, because, each time, we've moved to a
place where we knew no one. And often I was left
alone to look after our three little boys while my
husband, Ross, had to go on business trips. Yet the Lord
showed His faithfulness with every relocation, as He
watched over our family and went through every trial
with us.

On our first move, our four-year-old son had terrible
headaches. The diagnosis was a brain tumor, epilepsy, or
mental retardation. I'm thankful it turned out to be none
of these, and today our son is a healthy daddy himself.

Another episode God took us through involved a fire
in our home, in the middle of which my son took my
hands and said, "Mom, let's pray." I agreed, but
suggested we do it outside. Praise God, no one was hurt.

Next came a robbery, and, though I foolishly went
into the house alone, I was unharmed. The robbers were
caught, one in possession of my husband's camera. The

thief had already made plans to give it to his wife for Christmas.

On another move, my only, dear brother went home to be with the Lord, but I was able to be there when I was needed. All my trips of thousands of miles on many aircraft were made safely, thanks again to God's protection.

I am learning that in each place God takes me there will be a hurt, but there will also be an open door to exciting possibilities I've never dreamed of. This last open door was the chance to work with the street people of my city. I know wherever God takes me, He will go too.

Dear Lord, thank You for taking me places I didn't want to go and for helping me to become a better, rather than a bitter, person as a result. Continue to teach me more love for others and for You. Amen.

Joan Martin has published over 450 articles in a variety of publications. She enjoys crafts and knitting and is a speaker for Christian Women's Clubs. Joan is also involved in the Friend to Friend program, where she visits a woman in prison. She and her husband, Ross, have three sons and reside in Wayzata, Minnesota.

Moth by Mouth

Jeanie Maxwell

Make a joyful noise unto the Lord, all ye lands. Psalm 100:1, *KJV*

"Ouch!" A painful cry came as I fell from the rickety old sawhorse; coming down, I had cut my leg on a nail. To make matters worse, when I cried out, I swallowed a moth.

My mother was inside our church, teaching the Girls' Mission Meeting. I wasn't old enough to attend, and, obviously, my brother couldn't go, so we had decided to spy on her class by peering through the window.

My brother had taken his turn at spying; then it was mine. Everything would have been alright, except the old sawhorse gave out on me and I came tumbling down.

The nail scrape was nothing compared to swallowing that moth. I still shudder to think how it tasted.

From then on, I got to prematurely attend the Girls' Mission Meetings. At the first meeting I attended, we were encouraged to memorize Psalm 100. Since then, it has always been my favorite.

In the first verse, we are told to make a joyful noise. It may not have been a joyful noise that led to my memorizing this passage of Scripture, but the Lord has turned a lot of my painful times into joys ever since.

Father, may my attitudes be joyful even in difficult situations. Amen.

Jeanie Maxwell is the author of numerous articles and poems. She is a registered nurse and enjoys crafts, sewing, singing, teaching Bible studies, and swimming. Jeanie and her husband, Dan, have two children and make their home in Oklahoma City, Oklahoma.

Beloved Boundaries

Rhonda McGarrah

The boundary lines have fallen for me in
pleasant places; surely I have a delightful
inheritance. Psalm 16:6, *NIV*

It was a beautiful summer morning.
My two daughters had gotten up, dressed quickly,
cleaned up their rooms, and were already outside
playing.

I glanced out the family room window to check on
them. They were enjoying themselves so much, I found
myself smiling as I sat down on the couch to watch. The
object of their fascination was an imaginary playhouse in
our avocado trees, a playhouse that was entered into by
a real door.

The afternoon before, the girls had begged their
daddy to build them a house. Not being much of a
carpenter, he convinced them all they needed was a
door; then the rest of the open area behind it could be
whatever kind of house they wanted. So he proceeded to
put a metal dowl in the ground, nailed together some old
two-by-fours, and then attached this very crude gate-
looking door to the dowl so that it swung open and shut.
The children were delighted.

Now, as I watched them play, I noticed something

intriguing. No matter how many times they went in or out of their house, they always used the door. There were no walls of any kind to keep them from running around the door, but their daddy had said, "This is the way in and out and here are the boundaries." They took his word for it, and they didn't deviate from what he had set up for them.

If only I will walk through the open doors my heavenly Father has for me and stay within His boundaries for my life, by the leading of His Spirit and through prayer and study of His Word, I can be as content with His plan as my own little girls are with their daddy's plan.

Lord, You love me more than anyone else and always have the best plan, so please help me to trust You enough to stay within the loving boundaries You have established for my life, even when it's hard. Amen.

Rhonda McGarrah has had several articles published and is on the Advisory Board for the Crisis Pregnancy Center in her area. She has led home Bible studies and enjoys snow skiing, tennis, and family camping. Rhonda and her husband, Bill, have three children and reside in Ventura, California.

Out of Line

Cheri Metteer

Behold, Thou dost desire truth in the
innermost being, and in the hidden part
Thou wilt make me know wisdom.
Psalm 51:6, *NASB*

Only twenty minutes left and I could go home! I had put in a long, and hectic, Saturday on my job as cashier in a large variety store. It was three weeks before Christmas and the line was so long I couldn't see the end of it. It had been like this all day. My feet ached, and I was tired. It seemed like every customer was in a hurry. I tried to keep moving as fast as I could, but the pressure was getting the best of me.

Suddenly, a young woman appeared at my checkstand. "I had to wait in line at the customer service desk for half an hour," she told me, in a complaining tone of voice. "I'm only buying this one item, and I'm paying cash. Will you please let me pay for it here? I don't want to have to stand in line again."

It seemed easier to go ahead and wait on her than to argue with her, but when I handed her the change and receipt, the next customer in line remarked to her companion, "I don't believe it! Here we've been waiting in this long line and she lets that woman in ahead of all of us!"

"Hey! She's right, it's unfair! We don't like waiting in line either. She should have been forced to go to the end of the line like the rest of us!" snapped the next man waiting. I realized too late I'd made a mistake in helping this woman.

I started to defend myself, but the Lord prompted me to simply say to the angry customers, "I handled that situation very badly. Please forgive me."

The irate customers suddenly calmed down and smiled. Things quickly became peaceful again. What a difference it made to answer with a soft voice and humble spirit.

Thank You, Lord, for Your prompting and for showing me what a difference it makes when I ask forgiveness and respond in humility. Please help me to exercise godly wisdom at all times, especially when I'm tired! Amen.

Cheri Metteer has published in previous devotionals. Besides writing, she enjoys Bible study and journaling. She and her husband, Chuck, have five children and make their home in Kirkland, Washington.

God Runs
the Army

Dorothy Miller

*I will say of the Lord, "He is my refuge and
my fortress; my God, in Him will I trust."*
Psalm 91:2, *NKJV*

After years of telling others to trust
God, could I trust Him now?

Three years ago, Tom and I married and purchased a
chicken ranch from my parents. Both of us were needed
to work the ranch, so when the army sent a draft notice
to Tom, we quickly applied for a hardship deferment.
While we waited for a reply, Tom took, and easily
passed, the required army physical. Shortly afterwards,
he received a one-year deferment. We praised God for
this answer.

When the year was over, Tom received another draft
letter. We wrote to explain that the situation with our
ranch had not changed. We reminded them that since my
parents were elderly, defaulting on our payments would
hurt two families. We had confidently prayed about the

211

situation, so we were shocked when the deferment was denied. The letter said, "Be at Army headquarters in Los Angeles at 12:00, August 8. Bring only a toothbrush."

Now I was alone, wondering what to do. Just this morning, I had said a tearful good-bye to Tom. Certainly, God could see our plight. What had happened? I had been so sure God would change the army's mind. Even the day before Tom had to report, we had both expected a reprieve. It didn't come. Knowing that I couldn't survive at the ranch alone, I sat at the kitchen table, dazed and feeling empty.

The Psalm that I had just memorized with my junior-high Pioneer Girls came to mind. The words, "In Him will I trust," seemed to be a message from God. I prayed, "God, this whole situation doesn't make sense to me, but I realize that You're trustworthy. I've never had to trust You this much before. I suppose if we lose the ranch You have other plans for us. Please show me what to do; and take care of my parents, too."

I'll never forget the next few moments. Right after that prayer, the phone rang. It was Tom. "Dot, come get me."

"What?" I fumbled.

"Come get me. I failed the physical."

"But you can't have failed the physical; you've already passed it once." I was dumbfounded. Suddenly, I realized what had just happened. God wanted us to trust Him when the situation seemed impossible. As soon as I confessed my utter helplessness and said, "It's okay, God," He miraculously brought my husband home.

We never did determine why an army doctor suddenly discovered a "curve" in Tom's spine. *Why* didn't matter. What we did determine was that God had stretched our faith, and it felt good.

Dear God, You are so patient with us. Help me to

remember to trust You even when the situation appears impossible. Amen.

Dorothy Miller has written the book *White Unto Harvest.* She is a professional English riding instructor, bowler, home Bible study teacher, and leader of a children's musical troupe. Dorothy and her husband, Tom, have two children and reside in Covina, California.

God Is Smiling at Me?

Kathy Collard Miller

*Thou wilt make known to me the path of
life; In thy presence is fulness of joy; In Thy
right hand there are pleasures forever.*
Psalm 16:11, *NASB*

My sister-in-law Leslie said to me,
"Kathy, you'll never guess what Chuck said about our
Bible study the other night after you left our house."

I cringed inside wondering what my brother Chuck
might have said since he didn't come to the study. "Oh,
what?"

"He said, 'Boy, you guys sure laughed a lot.'"

I smiled. "Leslie, you should have told him, 'Kathy
was nice to us tonight; she let us get off our knees for
once.'"

Chuck couldn't believe that we could have so much
fun studying the Bible. Similarly, some people find it
hard to believe that God is joyful.

I've been in that category at times. Because of my
serious nature, as a child, I envisioned God as a strict
taskmaster who was always frowning and saying, "You
should have done better." But in the last several years, it's
been easier for me to think of God as being joyful—and
actually smiling!

I enjoy the story told by Pastor Paul Lee Tan about the children in his congregation coming into the morning worship service with their parents. When it was time for them to go to their Sunday School classrooms, they would march past the pulpit.

Pastor Tan said, "For me as their pastor, one of the high points of the service was the privilege of catching a smile from each child and giving one in return. I tried never to miss a single one, but one day apparently I failed. A little curly-headed four-year-old ran out of the procession and threw herself into the arms of her mother, sobbing as though her heart was broken."

After the service Pastor Tan asked the mother what had happened. She replied that when she had quieted her little one and asked why she had cried, she received this pathetic answer. "I smiled at God, but he didn't smile back at me!"

Whenever you feel like God isn't smiling at you, consider His Word, "In Thy presence is fulness of joy." That says to me that we have a God who loves to smile!

Joyous Father, I rejoice in Your presence, which is full of joy. I can be assured that You're smiling down on me and want to bless me with abundant life and pleasures. Amen.

Kathy Collard Miller is the author of four books and is a frequent speaker at women's retreats. Besides writing, Kathy enjoys bowling. She and her husband, Larry, have two children and make their home in Placentia, California.

Petitions With No Perimeters

Marjorie Miller

*I lift up my eyes to the hills—where does my
help come from? My help comes from the
Lord, the Maker of heaven and earth.*
Psalm 121:1-2, *NIV*

A preschool teacher had just told
the children they could talk to God anytime, anywhere.
As they walked around the yard for their wiggling time,
little Jennie noticed a lone daffodil in bloom.

"Teacher! Teacher! Look!" Jennie exclaimed. "Here's
God's telephone. Let's stop and talk to Him right now!"

We never outgrow our need to talk to God. And isn't
it wonderful to know that He is always available? In the
Apostle Paul's closing remarks to the Philippians, he
reminded them, "God will meet all your needs according
to his glorious riches in Christ Jesus." Paul wanted the
Philippian Christians to have the same freedom from
anxiety that he had. For although he was often in prison,
in want, or sick and alone, he had absolute confidence
that God was able and willing to take care of him.

This raises a couple of questions: What constitutes
need? And what concerns should we turn over to God?
Some people think that because they name the name of
God, He should relieve them of all sorrow and pain.

216

Others believe that we should reserve our cries for help for only the most extreme problems and not bother God with the little things.

God, in His infinite wisdom and love, has not established perimeters for our petitions. He sets no time limits on our prayers. But when we regularly spend time with Him in thanksgiving, in confession, and in supplication for others; when we submit our wills to His, then when we call on Him for help, He responds with blessings far beyond what we ask.

Where does my help come from? My help comes from the Lord, the Maker of heaven and earth. He will watch over my life...both now and forevermore.

Thank You, God, for supplying not only my needs, but countless numbers of my wants as well. Help me to trust You more. Amen.

Marjorie Miller has written curriculum, devotionals, children's books, and dozens of articles. From 1963 to 1989, she worked with Standard Publishing Company. Marjorie enjoys grandmothering, cooking, and conducting writers' classes. She has three children and resides in Mason, Ohio.

Hidden Life

Barbra Minar

*The Lord will accomplish what concerns
me; Thy lovingkindness, O Lord, is
everlasting; Do not forsake the works of
thy hands.* Psalm 138:8, *NASB*

After checking the lid on the yellow
juice cup, Lori placed her two-year-old's fingers around
the handle. She helped her tiny daughter tip the cup to
her mouth. "Good job, Megan!" Lori dabbed the dripping
apple juice from her child's chin.

Lori went back to her letter. "Longview High School
invites you to your Ten Year Class Reunion." *Ten years
already,* thought Lori, as she sifted through the pages.
"Please fill out the Personal Information sheet and return
to the reunion committee. What have you accomplished?
This is your moment to catch your classmates up on your
education, career, interests, marriage, and children."

*I've put this off until it's almost too late to send in.
What can I say?* Lori wrote: Hartfort Junior College—
Associate Degree in art. *Graduation from junior college?
That's pretty dumb. I've never even sold one of my
drawings. And since Megan, I haven't had time for art.*
Married to David Owens for five years. *Can't write
having a perfect marriage. My marriage is good but hard.*

218

Do I say: Helped David start his upholstery business?
Doesn't sound too interesting. Daughter Megan Marie:
age two. *What can I say about Megan? How incredible*
she is? How special? Everyone thinks their baby is special.

Lord, I hate writing this. What am I doing with my
life? I had such big dreams, and I'm nobody. I'm just sort
of hidden—hidden with Megan. I can't go to this reunion.
All I've got to show for ten years is eight extra pounds.

Lori looked at the oven clock and put down her pen.
"It's time. Come on, Meg." Lifting Megan to the mat, Lori
bent over and buried kisses in the soft folds of her neck.
Megan giggled. Lori unlaced her special high top shoes
and slid the braces off her legs. Megan kicked her feet.
"Time for exercise!" Lori caught Megan's leg and slid her
hands gently over the muscles checking the progress.
"What a strong girl!"

"Me big!" announced Megan.

Lori looked at Megan. The moment seemed to freeze.
Then Lori smiled. *Oh, Lord, You know what You're doing*
with my life. Making me big too—in You.

Lord, help me trust You with my life. In my weakness You
make me strong. In the quiet, hidden places of life, You
work within me. Help me remember that my value is
found in You. Amen.

Barbra Minar has published devotionals, magazine articles, and
three books. She has been a pre-school director, teacher, art
consultant, professional storyteller, and Bible study leader. She
and her husband, Gary, have three grown children and live in
Solvang, California.

Draw Near to God

Shirley Mitchell

But it is good for me to draw near to God: I have put my trust in the Lord God, that I may declare all thy works. Psalm 73:28, *KJV*

Imprisoned by four sterile walls, I held on to my husband's warm kiss before he left the hospital.

I blinked back the tears, for the next morning my white silk negligee would be traded for a surgical gown. And the feminine fragrance I was wearing would be replaced with the odor of the operating room and medication.

But my mood changed from gloom to joy when I remembered that I had an intimate relationship with Jesus Christ. For the past twelve years I had nutured this relationship with a daily time of meditation and study of God's Holy Word. I had spent time in prayer, talking and listening to my Creator.

God is not some mystical power somewhere out in the universe. He's my best friend, Savior, and Lord. I trust Him completely. For this reason I could say, "Lord, if You are ready for me to come home, I am ready. But if You have more for me to do here on earth, I will be glad to stay."

Being intimate with God the Father, God the Son, and God the Holy Spirit gave me courage to face major surgery without fear.

Now I'm "fit as a fiddle." But, I would never have survived the anguish had I not drawn close to God and placed my entire trust in Him.

Lord, my desire is to draw closer to You every day. I choose to put my complete trust in You. Amen.

Shirley Mitchell has authored three books and writes a weekly newspaper column entitled "Lace Over Steel." She enjoys reading, writing, and traveling. Shirley and her husband, Jack, have three grown children and make their home in Albertville, Alabama.

Overtime

Linda Montoya

To Thee I lift up my eyes, O Thou who
art enthroned in the heavens!
Psalm 123:1, *NASB*

Just one kick and it would all be over.
The fans on both sides waited in nervous anticipation.
My daughter Melanie and her teammates of eight- and
nine-year-old girls had made it to the A.Y.S.O. regional
all-star soccer game in Santa Barbara. A win would mean
the team would go on to compete in the sectional
tournament.

The game had ended with the score tied one-to-one.
Now the girls were in the second overtime
period—*sudden-death* overtime.

Melanie was playing as a diamond, positioned behind
the forwards. She could go either way to help out. One of
her teammates had taken a shot that bounced off an
opposing player. Then it happened. Melanie was in the
right place at the right time. She took the shot. It went in!
The crowd went wild. With screams of ecstasy and tears
of joy, the team pounced on Melanie, hugging her,
slapping hands, and giving high fives. Our team had won
the game. Her coach ran from the sidelines to
congratulate his team and applaud his scoring player.

And then, Melanie's head rose above the crowd. Her eyes searched the throng of parents and friends. She saw him and, with sudden abandon, left her teammates and ran to be scooped up in her daddy's arms.

He was the one who'd spent hours coaching her and training her. He was the one who, at times, seemed to discipline her too harshly. But in her brief moment of glory, she ran to her father.

O Lord, often in moments of distress I lift my eyes to You. Gently remind me that in my moments of success, I need to look up to You and run to Your loving arms. Amen.

Linda Montoya is a speaker and a writer. She enjoys teaching Bible studies, reading, and inspirational and humorous speaking. Linda and her husband, Frank, have three daughters and make their home in Ventura, California.

Ketchup, Please!

Candy Morrison

*Thou dost know when I sit down and when
I rise up; Thou dost understand my thought
from afar.* Psalm 139:2, *NASB*

I approached the breakfast table with
caution. Dad was cooking. Which one of his concoctions
would we have to endure this morning? My worst
nightmare became a reality. The fried eggplant I had
learned to despise stared up at me from my plate.

Automatically, I reached for the ketchup and
smothered the eggplant with the tomato's rich,
overpowering sauce.

The noisy exhaust fan and open windows should
have served as a clue. The eggplant was burned. It was
his trademark, to burn breakfast. It was something we
four kids accepted and, with big gulps of milk, learned to
live with.

Raisins were added to the oatmeal in direct
proportion to how burnt it was. Likewise, honey was
generously spread on over-baked biscuits.

No matter what we poured on, scraped off, or picked
out, the bitter taste remained. We couldn't camouflage
Dad's mistakes. The degree of burn was irrelevent. If it's
burnt, you can taste it.

How many times in our Christian life do we use "sauces" to smother the truth?

It's easy to tell "little white lies." The phone caller believed you when you said your husband wasn't home. Your little girl seemed satisfied with your explanation; after all, it saved her from a broken heart. The grocery store won't miss the money you took when you paid for twelve doughnuts and mistakenly walked out with fourteen.

Will a little honey sweeten our mistakes? Will people notice? Do I fool anyone? Maybe myself.

God's palate is keenly aware and sensitive. He sees our hearts and tastes the bitterness of our mistakes. We can't hide our sins from God, no matter the degree.

Dear Lord, make my heart sensitive to even the smallest sin. I don't want to try to cover them up or hide them from You. Amen.

Candy Morrison enjoys collecting antiques, camping, fishing, traveling, and counted cross-stitch. She teaches Children's Church and Spark Club at her church, but above all says that she loves being with her husband and three young boys. The Morrisons make their home in Roy, Washington.

"Not Yet" Faith

Geraldine Nicholas

Wait on the Lord: be of good courage, and
he shall strengthen thine heart: wait, I say,
on the Lord. Psalm 27:14, *KJV*

She opened her tiny fist to show her Grandma the four shiny quarters that had been given to her.

"What are you going to do with the money?" Grandma inquired.

"I'm going to put it in my purse," came the quick reply.

"Oh!" Grandma sounded surprised. "I didn't know you had a purse, dear."

"I don't," she replied emphatically. "Not yet!"

Turning away, she skipped happily off to her room to find a place to put her quarters in the meantime.

It was several months later that she opened a birthday gift from her grandma. Her eyes danced with delight as she exclaimed, "Look, Mommy, this is the exact purse I wanted!" The wrapping paper fell to the floor as she dashed away with the purse to find her quarters.

I think that God would be pleased for His children to exercise "not yet" faith when waiting is involved in prayer answers. I remember times when I have talked to God about concerns that were important to me. Sometimes there have been significant delays before He provided an answer or insight into a solution. Sometimes I have become quite anxious in the process of waiting. I've even resorted to questioning God with "why" or "when" rather than waiting patiently for an answer. In the midst of those times, He has brought to my remembrance my little daughter's uncomplicated "not yet" faith and reminded me again that the answer *will come*, in His time.

Help me to accept Your timing in my walk with You, Lord. Give me a trust that never doubts the delays You allow, but rather practices "not yet" faith until the answer comes. Amen.

Geraldine Nicholas has had poetry, devotions, articles, and short stories published in numerous publications. Besides writing, she enjoys reading, decorating, and crafts. She is Director of Children's Services at her local YWCA. Geraldine and her husband, Don, have three children and reside in Edmonton, Alberta, Canada.

Impatient... Who, Me?

Dorothea Marvin Nyberg

Don't be impatient. Wait for the Lord, and
he will come and save you! Be brave,
stouthearted and courageous. Yes, wait and
he will help you. Psalm 27:14, *TLB*

Impatient? Me? Never!

My husband and children wouldn't agree with that claim...and I have to admit they're probably right.

Some years ago, our youngest son and his wife invited us to go bike-riding. They had purchased new bikes and wanted us to use the old ones before they were sold.

Why waste time wondering *should we*? My reply: "Let's go!"

Off we pedaled. I was in the lead. As we puffed our way up a hill, my husband, Don, who was directly in back of me, hollered, "Hey, be careful; there's a car coming behind us!"

It passed. I swung back unto the road for the downhill sweep, shot ahead of them until...suddenly, my bike hit an obstruction in the road and stopped dead. I flew sixty-four feet through the air and made a three-point landing: two elbows and my jaw. The result was all three bones were broken.

Impatient? Not me!

Then why did I streak off ahead of them? That is a mute question.

Through the weeks of pain, hunger (due to a wired-shut jaw), and suffering, God taught me a lesson: Slow down, pause, think! A little patience goes a long way.

Father, thank You for the many lessons You've taught me through the years. Help me to be more patient with each passing day. And help me to mirror Your patience to others. Amen.

Dorothea Marvin Nyberg has authored three books and numerous articles. Besides writing, she enjoys reading, sewing, knitting, and walking. She and Don, her husband of forty-seven years, make their home in Olympia, Washington.

My Tiny Wooden Cup

Glenda Palmer

*Yea, though I walk through the valley of the
shadow of death, I will fear no evil: for thou
art with me.* Psalm 23:4, *KJV*

A tiny wooden communion cup—a
new gift—sits on my nightstand, and each night when I
go to bed, I am reminded of God's presence.

A few weeks ago, our twenty-three-year-old son
underwent surgery. The medical diagnosis: *cancer, not
completely removed.*

Within a few days, his room was crowded with
flowers and cards and caring, praying friends. My prayer
partner sent a "heal"ium balloon to him.

What an encouragement my prayer partner was! She
gave me some powerful Scriptures which spoke to me of
the all-sufficiency of Christ. She also gave me the little
wooden communion cup with this note from another
friend attached:

*"In Christ, your child is my child and I shall shelter
him in prayer as if he were my own. We are joining in
communion for him each evening. The wee cup is your
symbol of the covenant. You know of my love for you. Call
anytime. I will not call you at present, but I will call to
God, who gives wisdom."*

A few days later, several people gathered in our living room to anoint our son with oil and pray for his healing. My tiny wooden cup held the olive oil we used.

We have joined the fellowship of Christ's suffering. When so many of His children are crying out, "Abba, Father," I know He hears us, and I know He is able. Our son is God's child. I am His child too. Our cups are empty, but He is able to fill them. He alone is able. To Him be the glory.

Father, Abba Father, fill my empty cup with Your love. By the mighty power of Your Holy Spirit and in the name of Your Son, Jesus. Amen.

Glenda Palmer has authored several articles and poems. She enjoys motorhome camping at the beach and in the mountains. She is currently writing a children's picture book with songs and is a board member of the San Diego Christian Writers Guild. Glenda and her husband, Dick, have two grown sons and live in El Cajon, California.

The Beachcomber

Margaret Parker

He does not treat us as our sins deserve.
Psalm 103:10, *NIV*

Crashing waves sounded loud in our ears and the surf sometimes licked at our feet, but our eyes stayed focused intently downward. We were looking for seashells.

It was obvious to me that this beach had been thoroughly picked over. I wasn't finding anything worth keeping. But my daughter was discovering one treasure after another. Soon her hands could no longer hold them, and she put them in my beach hat for safekeeping.

I looked condescendingly at her collection. There were a few intact shells, but they were all small and ordinary.

Mostly, there were bits and pieces of shell. It seemed my child was determined to save every broken remnant that had ever housed a sea creature. When, I wondered, would she learn to be more discriminating?

Unaware of my jaded attitude, she thrust each new prize under my nose to be admired. I began to see them with her eyes. Some glowed with delicate pastel hues. Others had precisely sculpted bumps and ridges. A few were broken in such a way that their spiraling cores were exposed. As my daughter washed each one in the foaming surf, its unique loveliness showed through more clearly.

Jesus, I thought, *is a beachcomber.* He finds humanity washed up, battered, stranded by sinfulness. What if He chose to comb the sands as I do, holding out for wholeness and perfection? We would all be lost.

Instead, He moves among us just as my daughter combs the beach. No matter how often we have been rejected by others, He sees us as special treasures. He wants to pick us up, wash us off, and keep us close to Him. If we respond to His love, we will be surprised to see the beauty and worth He reveals in each one of us, in spite of our brokenness.

Precious Savior, Your forgiveness washing over me makes me feel so special, so loved. Help me to look at others as You do, remembering that in Your sight they are special too. Amen.

Margaret Parker has authored many articles and meditations, as well as leaders' guides and curriculum. Margaret enjoys encouraging and guiding new writers, and has led the Diablo Valley Christian Writers Group for several years. She and her husband, Bill, have one daughter and reside in Walnut Creek, California.

Seeing Clearly Through the Smog

Kathleen Parsa

Let us come before his presence with thanksgiving. Psalm 95:2, *KJV*

It was on the smoggiest day in six years that I received an unexpected letter from someone I loved; I wasn't prepared for its disturbing contents which hurt me deeply.

It was a letter of anger and resentment, of long bottled-up emotions, being vented in one huge explosion. I realized some of the accusations were valid, but most were not. The ones that were, I felt, were merely careless oversights, the result of my being insensitive. The accusations that were not valid left me feeling angry and confused.

Why hadn't I been told long ago? Why did she harbor her ill feelings to the point of becoming enraged? My initial response was that of self-pity and tears. However, in no time, I'd gathered my thoughts and purposed to write a letter. I knew I needed to pray first, but I had to make it quick, because the letter had to be written now, or so I thought.

"Lord, guide me," was the extent of my prayer. Then I began my letter by explaining my side, and, perceiving that she was in need of counseling (mine), I proceeded to instruct her on the fruits of the Spirit, particularly self-control, patience, and gentleness. After a time, I had to leave for an appointment.

While driving, I experienced blurry eyes, not only from my tears, but from the smog. "Oh, Lord," I prayed. "I feel so low, and this smog is awful! Lord, Your Word says to come before Your presence with thanksgiving, so I suppose I should be thankful. Okay, Lord, thank You for this day, even for the smog." And then it hit me. "Lord, do I have to thank You for the letter, too? Okay, Lord, thank You for the letter. *And the writer?* Lord, You mean it?"

I thought for a moment. "Yes, of course! Thank You, Jesus, for showing me so clearly...through the smog."

That evening I began my letter anew. This time the Lord would be in control: "Dear _____, Thank you for your letter. It was what I needed to bring me back down to earth. Much of what you said is true. I'm sorry if I've appeared flippant or disrespectful. I hope you will forgive me for being insensitive; I'm sorry you've been offended. I love you."

What peace flooded my dreams that night. Would the letter resolve the problems and rekindle our special relationship? I didn't know. But I did know I had listened to God, and with obedience came peace.

Thank You, Lord, for even honoring my teeth-gritting thankfulness. I love You. Amen.

Kathleen Parsa has had numerous articles published. She is a registered nurse and is interested in social and political concerns. Kathleen enjoys playing the guitar, decorating, gardening, and traveling with her family. She and her husband, Dar, have two children and reside in Ventura, California.

Cook, Don't Preach!

Marilyn Gaita Pellicane

*Your word is a lamp to my feet and a light
to my path.* Psalm 119:105, *NKJV*

A terrific message had come forth
this morning at Bible study. There had been so much
enlightenment and revelation that I was anxious to talk
with our college son. The Word and the message were
"so right" for him. The entire day I was planning our
conversation. God was giving me *hinds' feet in high
places* (Psalm 18:33) and I did so want my son to come
to know Him as a loving Father—One who can take
away the shadows and dark areas of life.

Dinnertime was drawing near and the excitement of
seeing and "sharing" with my son was overwhelming. At
the kitchen sink, as I was cleaning the last of the
vegetables, the Lord pressed upon my spirit the word
cook.

Cook? Well, I was doing that. I enjoy the culinary art
passed down from my Austrian/Hungarian mother. "But,
Lord, in what context, cook?" Distressed, I asked, "Give
me the mind and heart of God...not my will but Your
will." Clearly, the answer came, "Cook, don't preach!"
Sadly, I received the revelation that I was to cook for
John and not share the Word with him. Now, my

236

protective defenses were up. "Who is going to teach John the Word of God? Who, Lord, who?"

Lovingly, He said, "Not you. You are to cook for John." The Lord wanted me to shift gears; was I willing to listen? Was I voluntarily going to put my exhilaration aside and do the will of the Father? Crestfallen, I obeyed, reluntantly at first, but God began to delight my soul.

To this day I am cooking for John whenever he comes home. The Lord has shown me in His Word that John "shall be like a tree planted by the rivers of water, that brings forth its fruit in its season, whose leaf also shall not wither; and whatever he does shall prosper" (Psalm 1:3).

Trusting in His Word, I know that He will send His laborers across my son's path. God's Word will be a lamp to John's feet and a light to John's path. I need only to cook!

Thank You, Father, for reminding me that You have a plan for my life and for those I love. Help me to know when to speak and when to cook! I love You. Amen.

Marilyn Gaita Pellicane, besides writing, enjoys speaking for Women's Aglow Fellowship International and working in her husband's office as medical administrator. Marilyn and her husband, Arthur, have four grown children and live in Manhasset, New York.

Set Free

Laurie J. Perkins

*As far as the east is from the west, so far has
He removed our transgressions from us.*
Psalm 103:12, *NKJV*

It's hard for me to admit it, but there
have been times when I have doubted that God has
forgiven my sins. I feared He was disappointed in me. I
assumed that since I remembered it when someone else
hurt me, then God would remember my sins. I didn't
understand that when God cleansed my sins with the
precious blood of Jesus and gave me a new nature,
He covered me with Jesus' robe of righteousness
(Isaiah 61:10).

As I studied the Bible, His loving nature cleansed and
healed me. His voice changed, and it became more
gentle and kind. It helped me to personalize various
passages by inserting my name. For example, "And
Laurie He made alive, who was dead in trespasses and
sins" (Ephesians 2:1). What a change to believe in my
heart that God loved and forgave me.

With such a gift from God, I wanted to learn how to
forgive others so that I could overcome disappointments
and bitterness about my past. Many steps were taken to
forgive others, like ongoing personal and intercessory

prayers, guidance from the Bible, allowing the Holy Spirit to work in my life, calling on pastors and friends, and in my case, seeking the help of a professional counselor.

One of the biggest areas of change occurred when a pastor guided me in a prayer similar to the one below.

God continues to mold me. At times, I forget that He's in charge, and my feelings get hurt. But I am thankful for the joy and peace that have come from accepting God's forgiveness and in forgiving others.

Heavenly Father, I ask that You help me to forgive those who hurt me. Will You forgive them too? Fill me with Your Holy Spirit so that I can love them. Amen.

Laurie J. Perkins writes poetry and is studying short story and novel writing at USC. In addition, she enjoys Bible study, walking, and bird-watching. She and her husband, Terry, make their home in El Toro, California.

Peace After a Tantrum

Alice C. Peter

*The Lord is my shepherd; I have
everything I need.* Psalm 23:1, *TEV*

Tim is a frail, yet handsome, six-year-old with blond curls and dancing blue eyes. He is an active, demanding dynamo with spindly legs, threshing arms, and grasping fingers. His active mind spins like a machine, flies to conclusions, and often reacts before people around take in the scene. He expresses his love as quickly as his temper, and today he hugs his kitten as he smashes his brother's castle of wooden blocks.

"I can't build things like Tom does," he screams after his fleeing brother. "And I hate his model airplanes all over the place." He kicks the blocks and throws the cat.

"It's okay, Tim," I shout and try to hug him. He scurries away. "You don't have to do what Tom does. You don't even have to like what he has, but you can't destroy his toys."

Finally, I grab his flying hands and scoop him up in my arms. His body writhes with tension. His breath pants with rage. I carry him to his bedroom where Matchbox cars, plastic dinosaurs, and soldiers clutter the floor, competing for space with dirty clothes, sneakers, schoolbooks, and papers.

"Let's get you settled down and I'll tell you a story." I plop my squirming bundle of excessive energy onto his bed and wipe his tears. I hold his bouncing head on his pillow. Slowly his flailing ceases as I pat his curls and rub my hands up and down his spine.

I talk about David, the shepherd boy, caring for his father's sheep outside of Bethlehem. My words soothe Tim. David and his lyre bring calm to Tim's turbulence and peace to his limbs. Soon we are saying Psalm 23 together.

Because the Lord is my shepherd, I have everything I need. Even the strength to cope with Tim's hyperactivity.

He leads me beside the still waters. "Tim, did you know sheep won't drink from a rushing stream? They seek quiet pools, just as you and I search for calmness after one of your outbursts."

He restores my sanity. Tim is quiet now; his eyes are heavy and his energy finally spent.

Even when walking through the dark valley of death. Maybe my valleys aren't so dark or despairing as to be near death, but Lord, I get so weary!

I will not be afraid. That's not always so. Tim's outbursts are so destructive and draining. Sometimes I fear that he will wear himself out and cease to exist.

But You are with me. It's the only way I get through my day. Being human, I want to cave in, give up, and break down.

My mind wanders through David's psalm to the words: *Surely goodness and love will follow me...and I will dwell in your house.* "Thank You, Lord," I sigh.

Forever! With that ending Tim sleeps. There is hope and peace for both of us.

Father, what more is there to say. Amen.

Alice C. Peter has authored numerous articles for publication. Alice has had cerebral palsy since birth, and says she feels God "leads my life and uses my disability for His purpose." She enjoys American history (Revolutionary era), travel, and studying life and customs of the Bible. Alice has three grown sons and resides in Seattle, Washington.

Perfect or Perfected?

Peggy Bell Poe

The Lord will perfect that which concerns me. Psalm 138:8, *NKJV*

My working friends tell me, "If only I could stay at home, I could do my cleaning during the day and spend more time with my children." I, in turn, envy them their wardrobes and the prestige accorded them as "Supermoms." Therefore, this verse quells my dissatisfaction and assuages the ache in my soul.

First, "The Lord will perfect *that which concerns me.*" When Peter asked the risen Jesus what would happen to the disciple John, Jesus said, "What is that to you? You follow me." (John 21:22). I must not be envious of my working friends' lives; to my own Master I stand or fall.

Second, "The Lord *will perfect* that which concerns me." *To perfect* means "to complete in all respects." *Perfect*, an adjective, not a verb, means "flawless." God is flawless; we are not. Before God created me, He had a purpose for my life. If I cooperate with Him, He is able to complete His life plan for me. I am not responsible for the results, just the effort.

Finally, "*The Lord* will perfect that which concerns me." I want to give God the glory for that which He accomplishes through me. If I brag about my wisdom, others may be impressed. But if I assert that wisdom can be assimilated by reading the Book of Proverbs, others may turn to the Bible. If I proclaim Jesus as the source of my abilities, others will be drawn to Him as He is lifted up.

Dear Daddy Father, help me not to look at my neighbor but to keep my eyes on You. Persuade me that the best is yet to come. Amen.

Peggy Bell Poe has served as a bilingual secretary with Wycliffe Bible Translators in Mexico City and with her husband in Mennonite church work in Pennsylvania. She enjoys crafts, sewing, and Bible study. Peggy and her husband, Gray, have two children and reside in Newnan, Georgia.

More Than the Sand?

Eugenia Price

If I should count them [God's thoughts of us]
they are more in number than the sand.
Psalm 139:18, *KJV*

I happen to live on an island. I don't
go to the beach anymore because it is developed almost
into the sea. But more than twenty years ago, when I first
moved here, my friend Joyce Blackburn and I spent
hours on the then restfully empty stretches of St. Simons
sand. Needless to say, we didn't try to count the grains.
There are too many. We would have been overwhelmed
by the effort. Anyone would.

Are God's thoughts of us that great in number? "They
are more in number than the sand."

Does that sound as though God is too busy to bother
with helping me figure out my bank balance? Or quiet
my mind when I am anxious? Does that sound as though
His time for me is limited in any way? Does it sound as
though He is able to concentrate on my need of the right
word for only a few minutes at a time? Does it sound as
though you are entitled to only a few minutes of His time
when you're afraid, as you may be right now, of what
lies ahead in this day? Of what *may* lie ahead in it? Does
that sound as though Almighty God is too busy with

cosmic problems to realize that you are in desperate need of Him today when you have to keep that difficult appointment? When you visit that nursing home, won't He know you're there needing His own words of comfort, of understanding?

Think about it. Even those who have never seen a beach know about sand.

Oh, God, thank You that nothing is too enormous for You to think about on my behalf, and nothing is too small. Amen.

Eugenia Price is the author of the bestselling *Savannah* series and several nonfiction titles including *Early Will I Seek Thee, The Burden Is Light, The Wider Place,* and *Just As I Am.* Of the many books she has written, all still remain in print. Eugenia writes from her home on St. Simons Island, Georgia.

How Sweet
It Is!

Deanie Remenak

*O taste and see that the Lord is good; how
blessed is the man who takes refuge in Him!*
Psalm 34:8, *NASB*

Recently my Bible reading, prayer
life, and spiritual walk had become less meaningful, dry,
the words gone as soon as I closed the book. I was
bored with radio Bible teachers I normally found
challenging and stimulating. Reading Christian books was
as tiresome and dry as the bran I eat dutifully for a
healthy breakfast. As a part-time clerk in a gospel book
shop, I had a problem! But not as serious as the one I
had as a follower of Jesus Christ.

The Lord suggested that I had grown fat. Could a
person actually read and study the Bible too much? I
began to see that many of us are overindulgent
Christians, behaving like gluttons at a banquet table,
heaping our spiritual plates high with all the good things
at our disposal. We rush through like hungry children at
a church potluck, so we can run back for more to make
sure we haven't missed anything good. A prominent
radio personality calls it "overexposure" to things of a
spiritual nature.

The Holy Spirit has taken responsibility for my

growth and maturity. He is the chief dietition who must balance my menu so that I am becoming conformed to the image of God's Son. I must follow His plan so that I develop wholesomely, not growing fat and flabby and insensitive to His leading and the hunger of others.

So, for an indefinite time at least, I will go on a scriptural diet, eating only small portions, but savoring every tidbit. Each morsel becomes a delight to my intellect and spirit as I meditate on its pristine beauty and draw deeply from its purity and living truth.

Dear Lord Jesus, thank You for opening my eyes to my over-indulgence and turning a bittersweet truth into a truly sweet appreciation of You and Your Goodness. Amen.

Deanie Remenak is a speaker for women's groups and a Sunday School teacher. She enjoys quilting, sewing, classical music, grandmothering, and ministering to the elderly. Deanie and her husband, Leo, have four grown children and reside in Port Orchard, Washington.

A Little
Heaven on
Earth

Carol Rischer

*In Thee, O Lord, I have taken refuge; Let me
never be ashamed.* Psalm 71:1, *NASB*

This summer was a dream come
true: Our family of five vacationed in Maui in celebration
of our twentieth wedding anniversary, and it was a little
taste of heaven.

During our stay, we met some of the "rich and
famous," whose life-styles include regular Maui breaks.
They seemed to have it all, especially one young mother
of two toddlers we met by the pool of our hotel. She had
all the world has to offer, including a nanny to care for
her daughters, a yacht, three vacation homes—even a
firm, tanned body. What more could anyone want?

As we talked, however, she began to see that the
teenagers in our family enjoy a different life-style from
the one she had known. No drugs? No partying? No pre-
marital sex? They liked vacationing with their parents?
Were we from another planet?

The girls told her how God has a better plan for their
lives and why their standards are set where they are.
After a few days of poolside chatting, during which my
girls continued to share their faith in Jesus Christ, Melissa
decided that although Christianity probably was not for

her, she would like this God for her daughters. She recalled to us her own teen years, during which she "sowed her share of wild oats." She wanted to spare her children the pain she had gone through.

God is a refuge for teens who want to escape the addictions of the world. He's also a refuge for moms searching for truths, sorting out values, and wanting to begin anew.

As beautiful as Maui is, it's nothing compared to the beauty that awaits us in heaven. And as glamorous and exciting as this world might seem, it only offers emptiness and addictions. Jesus came to earth so that we might have salvation from our sins and the sins of this world. We can find our refuge, our protection, in the Lord our God. We need to unashamedly share this truth with those we meet. They need more than this world has to offer. They need Jesus.

Father, thank You for the beauty of this earth. Thank You most of all for Yourself. You love me, You protect me, and You are my source of perfect joy. Help me to share Your love with those I meet. Amen.

Carol Rischer is the author of *Insights for Young Mothers*. She is a professional pianist, conference speaker, and former radio-show host. She, her husband, Paul, and their three daughters, are known as the Rischer Family Singers. They make their home in San Jose, California.

Wonderful Are Thy Works

Lei Loni Rodrigues

*For thou didst form my inward parts; Thou
didst weave me in my mother's womb. I will
give thanks to Thee, for I am fearfully and
wonderfully made; Wonderful are
Thy works.* Psalm 139:13-14, *NASB*

Every now and then, I invite the
Lord to go along with me on a journey through my past.
I call Him into my "secret place." Stored within this
secret place are my personal journals. Recorded on each
tear-stained page are my heart and my life. I invite Jesus
to come along with me, because He was there at each
entry.

He was there when my soul lay bare and broken
before Him. He was there when I cried out for healing.
As we journey through the archives of my life, I want
Him there to rejoice with me as I am reminded of His
love.

Today I invite you to come along, too, as I recall the

day He explained what I was not created to believe.

"September 10, 1987, 10:18 A.M.: Life, my life; I'm learning to accept myself. It has been made evident that I have no regard for who God made me to be. I strive to know more, to understand the whys and wherefores, but as I throw up my hands in utter frustration, it's as though God catches what I release and, at the same time, takes my upraised hands and gently puts them down at my side. Lovingly, He says, 'Thank you, my daughter. Now that you have given me your dangerous play toy, I can explain why I have taken it from you. The toy is called self-hatred.'"

God denies me the right to hate myself or my life. He gave me life as a gift and created me, not as a mean, cruel trick—not as a joke. He did not create me as a reminder that, "Anyone can make a mistake, even God!"

As I listen to His voice, He explains that before I learn the mystery of why I was created, I must first learn those things for which I was not created.

I was not created to hate myself or the life given me. Degrading the work of God is a despicable practice. I was not created to believe lies about my self-worth, nor to audibly speak those lies as if they were true. I was not created to be in a perpetual state of frustration. I was not created to wander this earth on a lifelong expedition searching for love, self-worth, and acceptance. I was not created to carry the guilt or the burden of the world, nor was I created to solve the conflicts of the ages. I was not created for any of these things. You see, my Lord showed me, on this glorious morning that I was created for His pleasure. God, the creator of the universe, created me—little me. Surely, I am fearfully and wonderfully made.

Dear Lord, once again I thank You for joining me as I walk through the rubble of my past. Thank You for creating the universe and all of its wonder. And thank You, Lord, for creating me. Amen.

Lei Loni Rodrigues writes poetry and devotions. In addition, she enjoys reading, singing, working on her computer, and learning to play tennis. Lei Loni has two children and makes her home in Hayward, California.

A Song in the Dark

Scotti Baker Rosa

Heal my soul; for I have sinned against thee.
Psalm 41:4, *KJV*

I never thought of myself as a statistic, but I am one. I'm one of the thousands who chose divorce during the 1980s, and I love the Lord.

The fact that the Church is being touched by divorce is all too real. Pastors, family, and friends struggle with trying to understand. The person going through divorce struggles with the same questions even though it may have been of their choice.

I know I grappled with the realization that I had violated my own standards, broken the trust of friends and family, but most of all, I had sinned against the Lord I loved. The internal conflict was overwhelming. I was engulfed in feelings of guilt, self-incrimination, and remorse.

I felt that so many doors were closed to me, and my heart swelled with the ache of that reality. But then I heard a still small voice say, "You are of value to Me," and the tightness in my throat subsided. Silently, I said, "Yes." The healing process had begun.

I learned we cannot continue to punish ourselves. God would have us move on, and the strength to do this is found in the Lord. He is the One who heals the anguishing pain in our soul, for our ultimate sin was against Him. It may take others time to learn how to respond to us anew, but no such barrier exists with God. Instead, He says to each one of us, "You are of value to Me. Come, and let Me restore you."

It takes resolve to return to the place that God has for us. But I found it a place of healing, as I realized I am still of value to Him, for I have the life of His Son Jesus.

Father, thank You that You heal and restore us as we acknowledge our sin against You. Help me to appreciate the value I have in Your eyes. As I grasp this truth, enlarge my heart to see others in this light. Amen.

Scotti Baker Rosa has traveled to nearly twenty countries throughout the world. She enjoys reading and writing, having recently graduated from UC Berkeley where she minored in creative writing. Scotti and her husband, Gene, have six children and make their home in Martinez, California.

Discerning His Design

Barbara Rouleau

I will bless the LORD at all times: his praise
shall continually be in my mouth.
Psalm 34:1, *KJV*

At Christmas, a dear friend sent me a small plaque she had made. It was of needlepoint in just two colors. On a neutral background appeared a series of irregular, block figures.

Puzzled, I studied their erratic shapes but failed to distinguish anything of much significance. Nevertheless, it was a gift of love from one who is dear to me, so I displayed it on a table in the living room.

From time to time, I looked at my plaque, trying to decipher those figures in red that leaped out at me from a beige background. But, try as I might to understand, they conveyed no message to me.

A few days later, as I sat across the room, I happened to look up and immediately saw clearly the name of JESUS. Previously, I had been looking at the background and had failed to see the true design of the piece.

Now when I look at that plaque, my eyes focus on the name of JESUS. I am reminded of His presence with me, His care for me, His example before me, and His sufficiency for my every need.

Too, I am reminded that the cares of this life are only the background against which my life for JESUS should stand out. If I permit my problems to dominate my thinking, I blot out His design for me.

Grant me the wisdom, dear Lord, I pray, to keep the name of JESUS ever before me. Amen.

Barbara Rouleau has published several articles. She enjoys being with her family, corresponding, painting, crafts, cooking, and reading. She and her husband have been married for fifty years. The Rouleaus make their home in Garden Grove, California, with their daughter.

My Chocolate Chip Cookie Lesson

Jane Rumph

*It is better to trust in the Lord than to put
confidence in man.* Psalm 118:8, *NKJV*

I stared at the cupboard again, as
though by my gaze the box I sought would materialize.

Still no brown sugar.

"I can't believe I didn't put brown sugar on my last
grocery list," I sputtered. Here it was late Saturday night,
and my batter of chocolate chip cookies for tomorrow's
birthday party sat half-finished.

"You idiot," I began to berate myself. "You knew you
were low on brown sugar after you made cookies last
week. Can't you keep up a simple grocery list?"

Then another inner voice joined the conversation.
"Calm down; why the tirade? It's not the end of the
world. Besides, you can add some molasses to regular
sugar and it'll taste fine."

As I continued to mix the batter using the substitutes, I
began to wonder at my internal rage. Since childhood I
had wrestled with a strong perfectionist streak. It made me
an organized person and helped me do many things well,
but left me overly disappointed when others fell short of
my standards. As a result, I lived by the motto, "If you
want something done right, you have to do it yourself."

However, I can see that this motto has betrayed me. Often I've refused help, out of fear someone else will mess things up. Consequently, I cut myself off from the mutual support of friends. In addition, I end up placing unfounded faith in my own competence. Failure brings self-loathing, because the only one I trust let me down.

I slid the first sheet of cookies into the oven, and the truth began to dawn. In my fallen humanness, I am no more trustworthy than others. If I can do anything well, it is only by the grace of God. And when I fail, I see ever more clearly that perfection and reliability come from God alone.

My mind turned to the brothers and sisters whose help I so often spurned. *Funny*, I thought, *if I learn to trust in God to meet my needs, I just might discover in these others a willingness—and an ability—to serve as God's faithful channels of His blessing. And as I stop laying such a burden of perfection on myself, I might find it easier to live with my own flaws.*

The aroma of fresh-baked chocolate chip cookies filled the kitchen, and as they cooled I sampled one.

It tasted fine.

Dear Lord, help me release my self-reliance. Teach me how to put my trust in You—and in the ones in whom Your Spirit lives. Amen.

Jane Rumph has written numerous articles and devotions. Besides writing, she enjoys reading, baking, traveling, music, and needlework. In addition, she volunteers for a crisis-intervention helpline. Jane and her husband, Dave, "are a cozy family of two." The Rumphs reside in Pasadena, California.

A Watch of Nightingales

Dee Sand

I will sing of the Lord's great love forever;
with my mouth I will make your faithfulness
known through all generations.
Psalm 89:1, *NIV*

A head-on collision on a rain-slick country road had killed the passenger in my sister Margaret's car. A helicopter rushed Margaret to Suburban Hospital's trauma center in Montgomery County, Maryland. Five hours of surgery and sixteen units of blood later, Margaret had beaten the odds and lived to be admitted to the hospital's intensive care unit. Her condition would remain critical for more than two weeks and the surgeon's prognosis was dismal.

As family members were notified, we mobilized our own intensive care unit. With the encouragement of the doctors and nursing staff, we set up a round-the-clock vigil at Margaret's bedside. We took turns sitting with Margaret, praying and conferring in the hospital lounge, and going back to the house to cook, visit the children, and sleep.

Days and nights became a blur of hours. Exhaustion drove us home, but the realization that Margaret could die drew us back to relieve the other watch before we were rested.

Margaret was a mass of tubes and gauze and beeping monitors. For hours we sat talking to her, praying over her, or just holding her hand and listening to the respirator.

Then, sometime in the predawn hours of the second day, I heard the clear, sweet voice of Mother singing a hymn we used to sing when I was a child. Her eyes glistened as she sang about the love and faithfulness of Christ. As Mother sang, the lines on Margaret's monitors grew more regular. Soon, others of us began to sing to her the hymns she knew and loved. Sometimes, it would be one lone voice in the quiet of the night; sometimes, simple two-part harmony. But every night, at least once, someone would sing.

We have a God who never slumbers nor sleeps, who is enthroned on the praises of His people, and whose mercy never ends. We called on the promises we knew from our loving God and Father, and He answered the cries of our aching hearts. Margaret did gain strength while we prayed and sang and waited.

Seven years have passed since that awful accident. Despite countless medical procedures, Margaret is a very vital and active part of our lives. Her recovery is a testimony to the Lord's great love.

Heavenly Father, thank You for the music of the heart and the power of praise. Help us not to take them lightly. Amen.

Dee Sand is a storyteller turned writer and enjoys writing and performing dramatic monologues about biblical characters. In addition, she likes to bake bread and embroider. Dee and her husband, Kevin, have two children and make their home in Philadelphia, Pennsylvania.

God's Language

Nellie C. Savicki

*Come, let us sing for joy to the Lord; let us
shout aloud to the Rock of our salvation.*
Psalm 95:1, *NIV*

God speaks to us in a language that
sings and swings in rhythm with the universe. I
discovered this one day when the words from the Psalms
began to sing to me.

The word *joy* was my first discovery. Joy transcends
happiness. Joy is God-given and does not depend on
happenings in our lives. It is one of God's special gifts.
Like streams of water cascading down a mountainside
swelling into rivers of living water, God fills my heart,
and I sing with joy. Joy is God's love dancing in my
heart.

The word *thanks* undergirds my relationship with
God. Unless I take time to thank God, my lips become
parched. How can I write or talk or live my best unless I
quench my thirst with the living water?

And then there's *discovery*. I don't need to fear
growing older, because discovery is forever. Discovery is
throwing a rock into a stream and watching the ever-
widening circles. That is how I continue to know about
my God and myself.

Creation is yet another word in God's musical language. God is our creator. He has given me a gift of words and the power to create. Creation is a gift of imagination—like patterns woven across threads on a loom. Creation is a cobweb transformed by jewels of dew or kissed by hoar frost.

Prayer is a word that reaches up, sings and cries for freedom. "Hear me, God!" my thoughts seem to escape. Tears mingled with praises are like spring rains that help me grow.

These five words give a spiritual dimension to my life: *joy, thanks, discovery, creation,* and *prayer.*

I delight in speaking and singing God's language. In the words of the Psalmist, "Come, let us sing for joy to the Lord; let us shout aloud to the Rock of our salvation."

Thank You, Lord, for teaching me to speak and understand Your language. Today, I want to sing for joy to You and shout aloud to the Rock of my salvation! Amen.

Nellie C. Savicki has written poetry and several articles. She enjoys needlepoint, travel, gardening, and church activities. She has two grown children and makes her home in Auburn, Washington.

Of Such Is the Kingdom

Joyce E. Schmedel

*Righteousness goes before him and prepares
the way for his steps.* Psalm 85:13, *NIV*

"How did you come to salvation
and adopt a Japanese child?" she asked.

"Those events are unrelated," I said.

"In God's kingdom, nothing is unrelated."

My thoughts returned to Japan where, in 1959, my
husband worked as a civilian with the military. We had
come intending to adopt a child, and since neither of us
knew God, adoption was a decision unrelated to Him.
Or so we thought.

We had visited a Hiroshima orphanage, where
children sat in rows of boxes. Our hearts melted at the
smile of one five-month-old girl, and for six months we
tried for her release.

Then the phone rang.

"We're bringing the child," said the social worker.

"No," I responded. "I'll pick her up."

"They'll only release her to a third party."

A blanketed bundle landed in my arms when I opened the door. When I had unwrapped my new baby, I found a face flushed with fever and covered with a rash. Blood oozed from her swollen eyes.

I rushed her to the hospital and learned she was under-nourished, severely dehydrated, and suffering from a violent case of measles and conjunctivitis. She was eleven months old and weighed eleven pounds.

"If she doesn't drink by three o'clock, we'll have to hospitalize her," said the doctor. Fortunately, God answered an uttered prayer at two-thirty when she took her first drink.

Later, I learned the orphanage had had a measles epidemic and had released the sick ones to stem the outbreak. Fearing I would refuse the baby when I saw her condition, they had insisted on the third-party arrangement.

For a year we struggled with snags in adoption procedures, the first of which was obtaining the signature of the birth mother, who had disappeared.

"You must return the child to the orphanage. The case is hopeless," said the social worker.

"I'll return her when I leave Japan," I replied.

Our time dwindled. Finally word came: The police had found the mother on a primitive island. My husband left me in Japan to finalize the papers, as I had received a month's reprieve on my visa. Racing the deadline, officials hand-carried documents back and forth.

Winging away from Japan, I smiled at the miracles that had enabled us to adopt the child who sat on my lap.

It was later, when we settled in Los Angeles and chose a church with members of Japanese descent, so that our little girl would know others of her background, that we learned of salvation through Jesus Christ.

Thank You, Lord, that You chose to use a tiny child, in

need of a home, to lead our steps to a church that would bring us to You. Truly, nothing in Your kingdom is unrelated. Amen.

Joyce E. Schmedel has written and published two plays. Besides writing, she enjoys pen and ink drawing, Bible study, and reading. She and her husband, John, have two grown children and make their home in Camarillo, California.

Along My Weed Patch

Kathy Scott

Let them be as the grass upon the housetops,
which withereth afore it groweth up.
Psalm 129:6, *KJV*

I never could pull a weed without remembering my father. He hated weeds in his lawn and employed, without pay, four "weed diggers" to get rid of them.

Every day during the growing season, we had to spend one half hour on the lawn digging weeds. Whenever a neighbor complimented Dad on his beautiful grass, I always wanted to stand and say, "Thank you very much," but he accepted the praise without a nod in our direction.

In addition to the amount of time we spent, my father had another rule about digging weeds: "Always use a weed digger. If you don't get the root, the weed will grow back again."

Now, the weeds along my fence were growing taller than the flowers. So, equipped with weed digger and gardening gloves, I headed to the backyard. The first weed I pulled came out so easily that it almost threw me off balance. I tugged on the second and it also came out, roots and all—without the use of a tool. I glanced heavenward and said, "See, Daddy, you can pull out the roots—if the ground is moist." It had rained the previous night.

The smell of a certain grass tweaked my nostrils. Where did the memory of that come from? Oh, yes, it was Sunday afternoon; four girls were rolling down the grassy lawn at the memorial park. What fun we had playing on the mounted cannons and picking violets by the stream.

By now, I had reached the end of the fence and had a bag full of weeds. I looked at my watch and was surprised to see that more than a half hour had passed. I had had a pleasant walk down memory lane in the tedium of a distasteful task.

Like weeds along the fence, negative events spring up in life. Will I allow them to grow or will I get rid of them?

I've learned to recognize weeds. When we had our first garden, the only things we knew about plants came from seed packets and a few well-meaning friends. We planted everything in neat, little rows and then came back each day to watch them grow. As the green shoots began to push forth, each plant had a weed that looked just like it. We often pulled the wrong one.

My father's rule of digging the weeds down to the roots thirty minutes a day was met with great reluctance, but the principle is valid for life: Regularly dig out the negative thoughts and actions, so they do not root and grow again.

I've learned not to dwell on the presence of weeds. Much of life is like a lovely garden. You plant seeds and bulbs; weeds spring up by themselves. In life, these may be unkind words or rude actions. If not careful, we can allow the weeds to block the beauty.

*Dear Heavenly Father: Help me to remember that when
the garden of life is overrun with weeds, there is no room
for productive fruits and blossoms to grow. Amen.*

Kathy Scott has published over a hundred and fifty articles in
some twenty publications. She is a news correspondent for
Lancaster Newspapers and has been writing professionally since
1986. Kathy and her husband, Robert, have two sons. The Scotts
make their home in Conestoga, Pennsylvania.

Sarah

Ingrid Shelton

*Evening and morning, and at noon, will I
pray, and cry aloud: and he shall hear
my voice.* Psalm 55:17, *KJV*

Quietly I knocked on Sarah's door.
No answer. "She's in her room. Just walk in," the nurse at
the desk of the rest home had told me. Yet I hesitated.
She might be resting and I didn't want to disturb her. But
then I slowly pushed the door open and peeked in.
Sarah was on her bed, her eyes closed.

I felt sorry for her. She was so alone and, at almost
eighty, must have felt useless. Bedridden, her fingers
bent from arthritis, she rarely left her room. *What's the
purpose of her life?* I wondered. *Wouldn't it be better if she
were with the Lord she obviously loves so much?*

I'd do my shopping first, then stop by later, I decided
as I stepped back.

I had first met Sarah when I was a college student.
She was the mother of my friend, Verna, at whose home
I had spent an unforgettable weekend. The highlight of
my stay was the family devotions, and what touched me
most had been the prayer time when everyone kneeled
and prayed for his own needs as well as for those of
family and friends. I was a new Christian and that was

the first time I had been in a home where Christ was worshiped. I was deeply impressed.

Over the years, our ways parted and I rarely saw Verna or her family. Sarah's five children were now spread over two continents, the closest daughter more than two thousand miles away from the rest home into which Sarah had moved after her husband's death. As the home was located in the town where I lived, I occasionally stopped by to see her.

Returning an hour later from my shopping trip, I again knocked at Sarah's door and listened for her invitation to enter. Greeted with nothing but silence, I stepped in. Sarah was still lying on her bed, her eyes still closed.

But now I heard her voice: "Praise You, Lord, for Your goodness. Thank You for Roy. Make him a blessing to his students. Please, watch over Linda. Let no sin rule in her life..."

Instantly, I realized why the Lord has left her on earth: Sarah is an intercessor. Perhaps that's why all her children and grandchildren are serving the Lord, some in full-time Christian ministry. And that's why she exudes peace and joy instead of bitterness and complaining. What an example and inspiration she is, still bringing forth fruit in her old age, drawing strength and comfort from the Lord.

Thank You, Lord, for allowing me to know a saint like Sarah. Help me to enter life's golden years as she has done, with a heart full of praise, serving You until the end. Amen.

Ingrid Shelton has written several youth books, stories, and articles. She enjoys puppetry, traveling, and reading. She and her husband, Philip, have one daughter and make their home in Abbotsford, British Columbia.

My Priorities Are Simple

Dorothy Sickal

Give me the desire to obey your laws rather than to get rich. Psalm 119:36, *TEV*

As I knelt to sponge up spilled milk, I was dreaming about a vacation at a northern lake. A vacation. That takes money of which we never seemed to have enough.

I remember my mother telling me that in twenty years she had never had a vacation. She should have, that's for certain. But she was a happy person. She loved the Lord. Her entire life was centered around her home, her children, my father, and her neighbors.

She worked in the garden, she sewed, she liked to play ball in the backyard, and for fun, she was a part-time salesperson in a local department store. If she ever thought about getting rich I never heard about it.

What are God's laws I am to obey? Are they grievous? One of them is to be content. Dream about pleasant things but not to the point of resentment if they are out of reach. Another is to rejoice always. That does not depend upon getting rich. Joy comes from within.

I am rich in the love of my family. Joy, contentment, love, health, and pleasures are not dependent upon being rich in this world's goods.

Lord, may the desires of my heart be balanced with gratitude for the enduring things in my life. Then I can be prepared to better appreciate a vacation if we can go. May any desire for riches be controlled by the laws of love. I know that gratitude and greed make incompatible roommates. Thank You, Lord. Keep my priorities straight. Amen.

Dorothy Sickal has written numerous articles and with her daughter Gloria Gaither authored the book *Hands Across the Seasons*. She enjoys oil painting, drama, prayer groups, and mothering. In addition, she has taught and counseled at several youth camps. Dorothy and her husband, Lee, have two daughters and make their home in Alexandria, Indiana.

Wee-Hour Reckonings

Elona Peters Siemsen

*You probe my heart and examine me
at night.* Psalm 17:3, *NIV*

So it goes. I work at the office; I
clean, wash, garden, shop. I write a letter; I visit Lucy and
Ethel (with zeal that prompts my kids to say, "Mom's
having her devotions"). Before my bedside lamp goes
out, I've studied English culture with Agatha Christie and
made another tomorrow-I-diet vow.

Sometimes the day's been OK and I've felt like a real
person instead of an underpaid domestic. Sometimes the
day's been grand: I've gone with my children and
discussed trials, triumphs, and tragedies over seven cups
of coffee, or I've shared with a friend a burden from my
woman-heart and felt understood.

But there are other days. Tasks tumble over tasks.
There's another spot on the carpet (dubbed Africa, for its
shape). Someone I don't like very much tells me the Lord
just gave them that house on Lake of Swans, and I'm
sweltering in mine on Mosquito Creek.

Something happens when I accumulate a lot of
earthbound days. Eventually, there comes a night when I
lie languishing, eyes wide open under their lids. The
clock chimes three, and, two hours later, three-thirty.

Soon I know: It's time for another wee-hour reckoning.

He's here. "I've had some quiet moments for you," He says. "You didn't take them."

"I hate Adam," I fume, "for giving me this toil curse!"

I hear Him smile, "Often, deep within earth toil, you can find kingdom work."

I never ask, "Master, where have You been?" because I know. He's been there, as always, waiting for one of His sheep to move closer.

During these reckonings, the people and events of my days unscramble. "Why, there's Your touch on this event! And that one! Yes, I treated her wrongly. I'll call her tomorrow."

Sometimes, my night Visitor says, as the clock chimes again, "Remember, you've made Me Master of your days *and* your nights." You're right, Lord.

Beginning to drift off, I think of something else. "Lord, I've been hurt. I worked so hard on that task, and they hardly noticed. That seems to be happening a lot. I'd sure like to be appreciated and loved."

I think He's moved closer. "Dear child," He says softly, "you *are* appreciated. You *are* loved."

That is enough. I sleep again.

Dear Father, help me to remember You are Lord of my days and nights. May I stay attuned to You always. Amen.

Elona Peters Siemsen enjoys painting, calligraphy, song-writing, gardening, animals, dreaming, and, of course, reading and writing. She and her husband, Armon, are members of Wycliffe Bible Translators and have lived in Korea and Papua New Guinea. The Siemsens have three grown children and reside in Whittier, California.

Angels Watching Over Me

Pat J. Sikora

*If you make the Most High your
dwelling...then no harm will befall you, no
disaster will come near your tent. For he
will command his angels concerning
you to guard you in all your ways.*
Psalm 91:9-11, *NIV*

For months, our nearly new car had
been stalling. But it happened so intermittently, I knew
taking it in for service would be useless. Then the engine
began knocking and stumbling, making the car almost
undrivable.

"Why now, Lord? You know I can't be without my car
this week!" I fumed. I was spending nearly an hour a day
driving my son to vacation Bible school. "Where are You
when I need You?"

This was one more evidence of my growing certainty
that God had gone on vacation and left me behind. My
time with Him had become a barren desert. In fact, when

I tried to meet the Lord each morning, I would fall asleep over my Bible and coffee. I just couldn't connect. It had been a long time since I had hit such a dry spot.

Just as I was leaving the dealer's service department, I remembered another minor problem. *I might as well have it checked out*, I thought. "By the way, sometimes when I brake, the car swerves a bit. It's been happening on and off for the past six months or so," I said as I left.

That afternoon, I got a call from the service manager. "Mrs. Sikora, the nuts that hold the K-frame to the steering mechanism are missing. That's why you're swerving. We've ordered a new K-frame, but that will take at least three days. The good news is that even though your car is out of warranty, the manufacturer will cover it—a $650 to $750 job! They've never seen this problem on such a new car."

When I asked about the engine-stalling problem, he said the car was so dangerous that he couldn't have his technicians test it until the K-frame was replaced. "You're lucky to be alive, Mrs. Sikora."

Then I realized that God had not been on vacation. In fact, His angels had been working overtime, securing that steering mechanism, as my son and I rushed along the freeway each day. He had allowed the engine problem to increase, motivating us to seek help. He had reminded me to mention the steering problem—something I had not remembered previously. He had given the technician the wisdom to find an unusual problem. And, He had caused the manufacturer to save us a major expense. No, God was not on vacation. He was very present and still my Refuge and Protector.

Thank You, Lord, for being so faithful. Thank You that even when I don't feel Your presence, I can be absolutely certain that You haven't forgotten me. You are indeed my dwelling place. Amen.

Pat J. Sikora has written several books and articles in the health care and inspirational markets. She is a Bible study leader, a speaker on time management, and, in her spare time, likes to read, travel, garden, sew, and cook. The Sikoras have one son and live in Redwood City, California.

My Pink Chair

Josephine Smith

*My soul finds rest in God alone; my
salvation comes from him. He alone is my
rock and my salvation; he is my fortress, I
will never be shaken.* Psalm 62:1-2, *NIV*

What could I do with this chair? It
had been around a long time and had withstood the
wear and tear of family life. But now I was changing my
furniture around and didn't have much room for the
chair. I moved it from room to room, but somehow it
always seemed to wind up back in my bedroom.

Memories were wrapped up in that old rocker. It
seemed like only yesterday my little ones were playing
hide-and-seek behind its pink skirt. The bedtime stories,
the sick child, the times of talking over problems with
teenagers, the tears shed over some problems difficult to
bear... That chair had witnessed many events in my now-
grown-and-moved-away family.

One day, as I moved the chair to clean behind it, I
gave in and sank into its comfortable folds. Tears begin
to flow. As my tired body relaxed, my eyelids closed. In
my dreams, I was once again holding my dear ones close
to my heart. One by one, my children walked down the
path of my memory, and, as they did, a new love took

shape in my heart for them. I could see them struggling, fighting life's battles, while I was safely nestled in the arms of my chair.

I awoke with a start. How long had I been asleep? I leaned back and began to talk to the Lord about my loved ones. One by one, I brought them to Him and placed them at His feet. Once again I committed them to His loving care. Before I realized it, the morning was gone. My house still had to be cleaned, but my soul was refreshed.

I no longer consider my pink chair a piece of furniture that makes housecleaning harder, for it now holds a very special place in my home—and in my heart. It has become my prayer chair, and I meet the Lord there every morning.

Thank You, Lord, for my pink chair and for the privilege of prayer. Amen.

Josephine Smith has written articles and poems. She enjoys painting, teaching Bible classes, and counseling. Josephine is the mother of three. She and her husband, George, make their home in Santa Maria, California.

Staying
Wonder-Full

Lou Ann Smith

*I will remember the works of the Lord: surely
I will remember thy wonders of old.*
Psalm 77:11, *KJV*

Fresh snowflakes on my tongue. I
tilted my head back and closed my eyes, trying to
retrieve a faded sparkle of wonder.

"Get Dad!" Dustin, my ten-year-old, exclaimed. "I'll
bet he's never seen anything this wonderful!"

It was Thanksgiving and we were vacationing in
South Lake Tahoe. At about 7 P.M., the children noticed
through the motel window that some fluffy flakes were
falling. They raced outside and forty-five minutes later
were still standing in the parking lot, mesmerized, as if
they were watching the greatest show on earth.

Maybe they were. The street lamps cast a shimmering
light against the flurries, making them into thousands of

tiny figure skaters in sparkling tutus.

The scene had captured the imaginations of our kids, born and raised in the snowless Sacramento area. They stood in awe.

"Honey?" I grinned at Kirby, who was snuggled up with a newspaper, motioning for me to close the door. "Your offspring want to know if you'd like to go out and look at the snow."

"Are you kidding?" Kirby lowered the paper and started telling me about the time his uncle had fallen from the roof of his Minnesota house while shoveling off the snow. We both had a million stories, as I had been raised in the snow country of the Allegheny Mountains of Pennsylvania. Talk about blizzards! Yet even though I had gotten lost in deep drifts and experienced frozen feet and cabin fever, it was hard to remember a time when, as a young girl, I wouldn't long for the first snowfall of the season. Then, when it finally came, my sister and I would sit at our window half the night gazing at the moonlight dancing on velvet white roof tops.

Back out on the balcony, I watched Jacque write her name on the hood of the car. Then with sweet abandon, Dustin ran over to a lawn area and flung himself down, giggling and rolling around.

How easy it is to lose the wonder. Rare pleasures and firsts are filled with sparkle, but if we let them slip away, it isn't easy to bring back the newness. When I opened my heart to Jesus, His love amazed me. With tears of love I would sing over and over, "The wonder of it all! The wonder of it all! Just to think that God loves me."

Could I ever lose that wonder? Would it be possible to forget the freshness of His gentle love raining on my soul?

No, I won't forget. Because He'll help me remember. I'll ask Him to.

Holy Spirit, fall gently on my heart. Never let me lose the wonder of You. Amen.

Lou Ann Smith has written three books and several articles and is a speaker for Christian Women's Clubs. She enjoys being a full-time homemaker, reading, singing, and "driving taxi" for her children. Lou Ann and her husband, Kirby, have a son and a daughter and make their home in Cameron Park, California.

God's Passion

Sharon Sterrenburg

For Thou, Lord, art good, and ready to
forgive, and abundant in lovingkindness to
all who call upon Thee. Psalm 86:5, *NASB*

Sunday Dear Diary: I blew it again.
Sometimes I wonder how God puts up with me. Here I
am, a staff member of the church, a teacher of the
women's Bible studies, and supposedly one of the
"older" women the Book of Titus assigns to teach the
younger, yet I opened my mouth this morning and out
came bitterness, criticism, and even a betrayal of trust.
How can I get up and teach others? How can I lead them
in prayer? What am I doing in a position of leadership?

Monday Dear Diary: Things didn't look much
brighter this morning. I woke up feeling like one big
bundle of failure—God seemed so far away. Then, after
breakfast, I opened the Bible to Psalm 86:5 and read,
"For Thou, Lord, art good and ready to forgive..." The
word *ready* stopped me like a red traffic light. "My
failure" is all I have been thinking about; this verse
sounds like that isn't an issue with God. In fact, it sounds
like He isn't surprised that I sin. Have I been focusing on
the wrong thing? I need to sleep on this one.

Tuesday Dear Diary: It's a new day! Finally, I am

beginning to understand this verse—God has a passion for forgiveness. He is not mad at me. He has not disqualified me from ministry. He has not even temporarily put me on the shelf. Instead, He has been waiting all along to let me know I am forgiven. What a lesson! It is not the number of times I fall down that count, but the number of times I get up.

Dear Father, thank You for always being ready to forgive. Help me to realize that forgiveness is Your part; my part is to come to You with a repentant heart and get up and start again. I've wasted three days in the "guilt closet;" help me to do better next time. Amen.

Sharon Sterrenburg has written several Bible studies and is a frequent retreat and seminar speaker. She enjoys traveling, quilting, and grandmothering. Sharon and her husband, Don, have two grown children and reside in La Mirada, California.

Which Pony, Lord?

Kay Stewart

*For Thou hast been my help! And in the
shadow of Thy wings I sing for joy.*
Psalm 63:7, *NASB*

Sometimes opportunity knocks in rounds.

I had prayed for creative time and opportunity to work on my writing and music. The day lay before me like a clean sheet of paper, yet I floundered. *Which pot shall I stir when all are boiling?* The more I tried to focus on a given task or project, the more rattled I became. Some writers get blocked and ideas won't form. I get stymied as the colorful possibilities of a kaleidoscope whirl through my brain. It's like choosing the pony on the carousel. All are moving. All are colorful. Which do I take? Which do I eliminate?

In a fit of desperation, I called Jessica. Faithful to pray, she came right over. We talked. We prayed. She left. My overworked brain was a sodden sponge—no form sprang forth in story, song, or devotion. The day, full of sun and shadows, beckoned me outdoors. I took my harp and sang and played in nature's beauty. My spirit rested. Strength and renewal began to filter through my soul. In the gentle prompting of the Lord, a song sprang forth. My husband, listening nearby, looked up from his reading.

"New?" he asked.

"Yes."

"Nice," he responded. The sound of something newly created cheered us both.

Could this have happened without the prayer, the Lord, and Jessica? I think not. My Lord provides all that I need, whatever the circumstances. Suspending my self-reliance in favor of Him produces good works and gives Him the glory.

Thank You, Lord, that You are with me in my weakness and confusion. Thank You for my heart and mind and for directing them for Your good purposes. Amen.

Kay Stewart has had several articles published. She plays the Irish folk harp and sings, performing with her husband, Don, and solo. Kay leads a writers' critique group and conducts a children's church choir. The Stewarts have five grown children and reside on Bainbridge Island, Washington.

A Morning of Imagination

Eileen Swymer

*O Lord, open my lips, and my mouth will
declare your praise.* Psalm 51:15, *NIV*

"But Moses, you've got an
appointment with the president in ten minutes!" a
squeaky voice floated from my family room.

"Can Barbie come, too?" came the just-as-squeaky
response.

I glanced up from my grocery list to watch my two
youngest children at play. An odd assortment of Barbie
dolls and action figures provided the cast of characters.
Ken, sitting behind the wheel of a pink plastic Corvette,
was filling in for Moses. Amused, I listened to an
assemblage of Sunday School lessons, television shows,
and current events wrapped up together in one morning
of imagination.

How neatly and easily all the pieces of their fantasy fit
together. There were no divisions between secular and
religious, fantasy and reality, or even between ancient
and current. Of course, that comes easy to a five- and a
three- year-old. I began to think about my own life. All
the pieces didn't fit together quite so neatly. Was I
making divisions that didn't need to be?

I have my secular friends and my church friends. With other Christians I readily share what God has done for me and how He has answered prayer. But over a cup of tea with a neighbor who does not know the Lord, I am much more likely to discuss the pros and cons of shopping in a particular supermarket.

My children have the right approach, I've decided, and I've learned something from them. I'm going to invite my church friends and my non-church friends over for lunch together. I can tell them *all* how God has been at work in my life. I think I'll start with the story of how Moses met the president.

Lord, thank You for the lessons You have taught me through my children. Now help me to put them into practice. Amen.

Eileen Swymer is a new writer, looking forward to a long career in free-lancing. She enjoys cross-stitch, reading, and carpooling. She and her husband, Stephen, have six children and make their home in Exton, Pennsylvania.

H-E-A-V-E-N

Corrie ten Boom

*O give thanks to the Lord, call on his name,
make known his deeds among the peoples!*
Psalm 105:1, *RSV*

My last stop on my first trip to the Orient was Formosa. It was time for me to move on so I went to the travel agency in Taipei and gave the girl a list of all the places I needed to go on the next leg of my journey. Hong Kong, Sydney, Auckland, then back to Sydney, on to Cape Town, Tel Aviv and finally to Amsterdam.

The travel agent wrote it all down and then asked, "What is your final destination?"

"Heaven," I answered simply.

She gave me a puzzled look. "How do you spell that?"

"H-E-A-V-E-N," I spelled out slowly.

After she had written it down she sat looking at the paper. At last she looked up, "Oh, now I understand," she said with a smile. "But I did not mean that."

"But I meant it," I said. "And you do not need to write it down because I already have my ticket."

"You have a ticket to *heaven?*" she asked, astonished. "How did you receive it?"

"About two thousand years ago," I said, noting her genuine interest, "there was One who bought my ticket for me. I only had to accept it from Him. His name is Jesus and He paid my fare when He died on the cross for my sins."

A Chinese clerk, working at the next desk, overheard our conversation and joined in. "What the old woman says is true," he told his companion.

I turned and looked at the Chinese man. "Have you a reservation for heaven?" I asked him.

His face lit up in a smile. "Yes, I have," he said, nodding enthusiastically. "Many years ago, as a child on the mainland, I received Jesus as my Saviour. That makes me a child of God with a place reserved in the house of the Father."

"Then you are also my brother," I said, shaking his hand. Turning back to the other clerk I said, "When you do not have a reservation for a seat on the plane, and try to get aboard, you face difficulty. But when you do not have a place reserved for you in heaven, and the time comes for you to go, you end up in far greater difficulty. I hope my young brother here will not rest until you have made your reservation in heaven."

The Chinese clerk smiled broadly, and nodded. I felt confident he would continue to witness to his fellow worker now that I had opened the door.

Father, thank You for reserving my place in heaven, and for opportunities to share my good fortune with others, inviting them to enter into eternal life too. Amen.

Corrie ten Boom's remarkable story of faith is told in the bestseller, *The Hiding Place*. Books by Corrie include *Amazing Love*, *A Prisoner and Yet*, *This Day Is the Lord's*, and *Tramp For the Lord*. She died in 1983, but not before she left an indelible mark on the hearts and lives of millions of people around the world.

Was It Really by Chance?

Sandy Thiese

We live within the shadow of the Almighty,
sheltered by the God who is above all gods.
Psalm 91:1, *TLB*

Before moving from Albuquerque, New Mexico, to southern New Jersey, a friend from church, who was seriously ill, suggested I meet her daughter who lived in New Jersey. I contacted her daughter Corene and we became instant friends.

One day, Corene called to tell me her mother had died and that she would be leaving for Albuquerque for an indefinite length of time. Before she returned and I could see her again, our family was transferred to Michigan, after only ten months in New Jersey. Since I was unsuccessful in my attempts to contact Corene, I thought I would probably never see her again.

Eighteen months later, we were transferred back to New Jersey, but this time we settled in the northwest corner of the state. As usual, soon after a relocation, we visited a local church and introduced ourselves to the pastor.

This move had been more difficult than most and I was feeling lonely. Mom, who was visiting and helping me unpack, expressed her hope that I would soon find some new friends, reminding me of the friendship I had had with Corene.

Just then, the doorbell rang. When I answered the door, a stranger greeted me by name. Suddenly, I realized the stranger was Corene. After spending hours talking non-stop, I learned that Corene and her family had visited the same church we had, and when the pastor learned of their many relocations he told them of a similar family—ours. Corene recognized our name instantly and asked for our address. Her family had moved from southern New Jersey to Iowa, then recently moved back to northern New Jersey, only ten miles away from our home. We have since remained close friends, even though many miles separate us once again.

Some events in our lives seem to be coincidental, but if we're open to God's presence in our lives, we realize that there are "God-incidences" that are too special and too important to have happened by chance.

Dear Lord, help me to trust and be open to Your promise that You are with me every moment of my life. Thank You for the "God-incidences" that happen in my life, even those I fail to recognize. Amen.

Sandy Thiese is a rehabilitation case manager. In addition, she volunteers in the Stephen Ministries in her church. Sandy enjoys gardening, taking long walks, and traveling with her family. She and her husband, Alan, have three children and make their home in Rochester Hills, Michigan.

Forget and Forgive

Susan F. Titus

But with you there is forgiveness.
Psalm 130:4, *NIV*

I saw her across the room, seated in the corner. Her glance caught mine, and she brushed a wisp of long, chestnut hair out of her eyes. She stared at me a moment, waiting for my reaction.

It had been so long since our paths had crossed, yet it seemed like yesterday. I thought I had forgiven her, but the old feelings of resentment and anger welled up inside of me, and my stomach churned over and over.

"She wronged me. I did nothing to her. She never said she was sorry or asked my forgiveness," I reminded myself. I wanted to rush up and shake her and shout, "Why aren't you sorry?" Instead, I simply stared back at her.

Unexpectedly, she stood up and walked towards me. I closed my eyes and said a silent prayer. When I opened them, she stood beside me.

Suddenly, I pictured her in a different light. She looked vulnerable, unsure. Had I overreacted? Was I rationalizing my own wrong attitude? Perhaps I hadn't truly forgiven her.

I smiled and said, "I'm glad you're here. It's been a

long time." And I genuinely meant those words. The built-up resentment and anger vanished with my prayer.

"I wasn't sure you'd want to see me again," she stammered.

"Let's forget the past," I offered. "How about a glass of lemonade?"

She looked relieved. A slight smile formed on her lips. For the first time, I realized how much that lack of forgiveness had cost us both.

Dear Lord, please help me not to allow resentment to build up in my heart. Teach me to forgive and forget. Amen.

Susan F. Titus has written numerous children's stories and curriculum materials and has published six books. Susan is associate director of the Biola University Writers Institute, a publishing consultant for Educational Ministries, and frequent speaker at writers conferences. She has two sons and resides in Fullerton, California.

Heart High on Tiptoe

Doris Toppen

*Teach me the way I should walk; for to Thee
I lift up my soul.* Psalm 143:8, *NASB*

I asked Jesus into my heart about the same time I learned to ride a bicycle—almost more than a young heart could contain. I was ten, and the world was filled with new beginnings.

Dad had traded his tools to get a bicycle for me in those tough Depression days. The best bargain was a huge relic with a ragged seat. "Daddy, it's perfect," I said.

The crisp air tickled my nose on that magical morning so long ago. And the succulent sting of damp earth, decaying blackberry vines, and Dad's aftershave registered the moment in my forever-memory file, as Dad propped me against the dirt bank on our dead-end street. When I heard the click as I pushed down on the pedals, something in me clicked, too—that sense of wonder and adventure that filled my world because Dad walked beside me.

For days, Dad held onto the bicycle seat and tirelessly encouraged and guided me up and down the road. Finally, I was able to balance and sailed off alone. As Dad let go, I lifted my face to the breeze and laughed up at the clouds, my heart high on tiptoe. "Daddy, I can do it," I called back.

"I knew you could, Dorrie," he said. And somehow Dad always made it to the end of the road to catch me and point me back up the incline toward home.

My heavenly Father, too, picks me up when I fall, encourages me to brush myself off and try again. I learn to miss some of the chuckholes and ride out the rest. And with God even familiar roads are exciting.

I remember most the intoxication of complete joy in those first days of maneuvering that bicycle—though scraped knees and bruises were a reality too. But, whether riding through mud, bouncing over gravel, or sailing on the smooth blacktop, warmed by lazy, afternoon sun, the delight was in the journey.

Today, as a grandmother, butterflies dance in me still whenever I remember the crunch of gravel beneath the tires of that rusty, junkyard bicycle. As I plan new beginnings, God shows me daily that I travel holy ground and meet my miracles on the road to becoming who I am. So, with head held high, I can face the winds, look up at the clouds, and sing, "Thank You, Father God. You are my guide. I know I can do it."

Lord God, thank You for going before me, to catch me when I fall, and to encourage me to ride again. And when I wobble and hesitate, You steer me forward to bright new beginnings. Amen.

Doris Toppen retired from her job as a dental assistant to write full time. She has published in a variety of publications and writes and directs plays for her church. She is an aerobic dance instructor and enjoys jogging, hiking, gardening, and reading. She and her husband, Harvey, have four grown children and reside in North Bend, Washington.

Secretarial Sahara

Tina Torres

He turned the desert into pools of water,
and the parched ground into flowing
springs. Psalm 107:35, *NIV*

"I can't take this job anymore, Lord!
Is this all I'm capable of?" My desperation was growing
that morning. I sensed, again, a total lack of satisfaction
in my work as a secretary. It was boring with a capital B,
and, to top it off, I felt hassled and unappreciated. I
couldn't move up without getting into another
department where there was more stress and lots of
overtime. As a single parent of a teenage daughter, I
didn't want that.

So here I was, at the bottom of the ladder in a male-
dominated company, doing piddling things that nobody
else wanted to bother with. There was no challenge, no
excitement, nothing to utilize abilities I knew God had
given me. I was busy, but with mundane, inane tasks.
"Lord, this is monotonous and meaningless. I just don't
want to be here!"

In the midst of all this, I remembered that Christians
are supposed to be different. We are not victims, no
matter what the circumstances. We are overcomers and
are meant to "reign in life." So what was I doing wrong?

Maybe I was just forgetting who I am in Christ—that I'm a child of God, that He loved me and died for me, and that He has a mission for me wherever I happen to be. And He is the God of transformation—He changed my life from darkness to light, and He can change my secretarial stagnation into a place of flowing springs where His Holy Spirit can fill me with a deep joy that defies explanation.

I am still asking the Lord whether I should change jobs. Meanwhile, though, I'm beginning to experience God's transforming power in my current situation. And that's what it's all about, isn't it?

Lord, please transform my personal desert into pools of water, my agitation into Your peace. And allow me to help other women who are going through this same wilderness, especially those who don't know You. Amen.

Tina Torres, besides writing, has been active in evangelism, missions, and women's ministries. She is a Spanish translator/ interpreter and lived in Mexico City for thirteen years. Tina has one son and one daughter and lives in Foster City, California.

Lessons in Trust

Peggy Trim

*Some trust in chariots, and some in horses:
but we will remember the name of the
Lord our God.* Psalm 20:7, *KJV*

Whenever I plan to drive any
distance without my husband, he checks the car so I will
have confidence it won't break down. But despite my
husband's conscientious efforts, I still grapple with the
question, *What will I do if the car breaks down?*

One hot July, when I was fifty miles from home with
three of my children, it happened: The car sputtered,
lurched, and coasted to a stop; I eased it to the shoulder
of the road. My lanky teenage son announced, "You're
supposed to lift the hood if you're in trouble."

"Go ahead," I muttered, as I contemplated my
dilemma and wondered, *Where is God?* Trying to keep
the uneasiness out of my voice, I instructed the kids,
"Pray a patrolman stops to help; I don't want just
anybody stopping."

One car swished by, then another. *God is near after
all,* I chuckled to myself as a patrol car approached from
the rear, its antennas waving a jolly hello.

"Need help, ma'am?"

"Sure do."

Soon a tow truck was on its way.

"Thanks," I smiled as the trooper prepared to leave. "We prayed a policeman would be the one to help us." He tipped his hat and drove off.

The very next week, as my two daughters and I were driving over the scenic Cascade Mountains, the car hesitated, sputtered, and died. "Not again so soon!" I groaned. We lifted the hood, then climbed back into the car and locked the doors behind us. My prayer this time was simply, "Help."

Soon a pickup parked behind us and the driver got out. I watched the young man's reflection suspiciously in the side-view mirror as he sauntered toward us. Our eyes locked as we peered at each other through the slit of my partially opened window. He bent closer for better visibility—or was it possibly for attack?

"Lady," he whispered. Automatically and breathlessly, I leaned toward the door as he continued, "I'm no mechanic, but I could send a tow truck."

"Thanks," exploded from my mouth, as air gushed from my bursting lungs. "I'd appreciate that. There's a station about ten miles ahead."

Feeling rather sheepish because of my unnecessary apprehensions, I decided to read my Bible while we waited. Randomly, I opened it. I wondered what God would have to say about this? There on the open page was one underlined verse, *Some trust in chariots, and some in horses: but we will remember the name of the Lord our God.*

Later, as we bumped along behind the tow truck, I couldn't help but realize how unnecessary all my worry had been. I had had many safe driving miles, but when I did have trouble, God had provided the solutions.

Lord, thank You for caring and helping in time of need.
Amen.

Peggy Trim has written for several publications. She enjoys knitting and reading. Peggy is a pastor's wife, mother of five grown children, and foster mother. The Trims make their home in Methow, Washington.

My Word
or His?

Ann Udell

*In God will I praise his word: in the Lord
will I praise his word.* Psalm 56:10, *KJV*

"Grandma, look what we made in
Sunday School," yelled our grandsons as they raced into
the sanctuary, trying to outtalk each other.

The gentle harmony of piano and organ, indicating
morning worship was about to begin, prompted me to
collect their papers, take their hands, and head for the
side exit. Attempting to soften their glee by lowering my
voice, I said, "Boys, it's time for junior church." Their
bubbly enthusiasm abruptly ended. Adam, five, declared
he was big enough to go by himself, while Aaron, three,
proclaimed he was not going without me. Any illusion of
quietly departing vanished.

Now, lunch was finished and the boys were napping.
The hectic morning was over; it was finally quiet. A
perfect time to read the Scriptures from the morning's
message, which I had missed.

A cursory search of the house failed to reveal my
Bible but did disclose a growing, uncomfortable yet
elusive feeling. I attempted to dispel the sensation by
locating another Bible and settling into my most
comfortable chair. As I turned the pages, trying to
concentrate, a name for my feelings emerged—anxiety.
What had begun as a slight gnawing had grown to full-
scale panic. My Bible, which contained all my special

notes, remarks, insights, prayer requests, and answers—all of which could not be replaced—was missing.

That particular Bible reflected my walk with God! What if, in the process of trying to discover who the Bible belonged to, someone looked through it? They would not only see my personal victories, but my struggles, doubts, and fears. Suddenly, I felt exposed and vulnerable.

The whirlwind rotating through my mind was interrupted with a question. "Which are you most concerned with, the loss of your words or the loss of my Word?" God had spoken.

I shuddered. My Bible was my most important book, but had I elevated this particular one above all others because it recorded so much of myself? Had I exalted my words above those of God?

With a heavy heart, I had to acknowledge that God had unerringly identified my problem and allowed this incident to reveal a part of myself and my relationship with Him that I had not seen before.

The silence broke as my husband came through the back door, his arms a jumble of jackets; coffee mugs dangled from his fingers. "Honey, I found your Bible under this stuff in the car," he said as he deposited the pile on the coffee table.

I smiled, kissed him, and said, "Thanks."

Father, please forgive me for elevating my words above Yours. Cause me to always remember there are no other words greater than Yours, because You are Your Word. Amen.

Ann Udell enjoys traveling, camping, cooking, gardening, interior decorating, and teaching women's Bible studies. Currently, she is president of the women's ministries at her church. Ann and her husband have three grown children and make their home in Atascadero, California.

Oceans of Love

Yvonne Unfreid

Restore to me the joy of Thy salvation,
and sustain me with a willing spirit.
Psalm 51:12, *NASB*

My granddaughter and I were romping in the surf off my favorite Southern California beach. I felt like a kid again, forgetting the aches and pains of middle age and ignoring the stares of young beauties with perfect figures. Their knowing smiles confirmed what I already knew—that my bathing suit bulged in all the wrong places and my legs resembled twin road maps.

I didn't care. I was reliving the best of my childhood alongside a pint-sized version of myself. Tara loved the ocean as much as I did.

As seven-year-olds often do, she struck up an instant friendship with a little girl from the Midwest who was seeing the ocean for the first time.

Tara was obviously enjoying her role a tour director and took great delight in showing her new friend how to dig for sand crabs and jump over the waves. Both girls giggled with delight.

I tried to imagine what it would be like to experience the surf for the first time. I realized that I had long since learned to take its joys for granted.

It had been too long since I had taken the time to search for the perfect seashell or to watch a tiny sand crab scurry around on the palm of my hand before letting it go.

It wasn't until I was on the freeway, heading for home with Tara sound asleep on the backseat, that I made the connection with my Christian walk.

How long had it been since I experienced the joy of sharing the delights of my faith with an unbelieving friend? I tried to remember how I felt when I first understood the price Christ had paid for my sins.

Like the ocean, God's love is just there and it becomes all to easy to accept it, to enjoy its benefits, and to lose the wonder.

Lord, help me to recapture the joy I felt when my faith was new. Amen.

Yvonne Unfreid, an elementary school secretary, spends most of her non-working hours writing devotions, articles, and fiction and has completed her first nonfiction book. Yvonne enjoys music, having a degree in vocal music from CSU, Los Angeles. She and her husband, Richard, have two married sons and make their home in La Mirada, California.

My Help
Is in God

Marcia Van't Land

I will lift up my eyes to the hills...My help comes from the Lord, the Maker of heaven and earth. Psalm 121:1-2, *NIV*

For four years now a friend and I have been memorizing portions of Scripture. We call each other on Fridays, and often I pick up the phone to hear, "This is your friendly conscience speaking."

At times, I'm not quite ready to recite my verses when she calls, so we hang up. I memorize the verses and call her back. Sometimes, she is the one who needs more time.

Often, I berate myself: *Why can't I memorize just two verses a week?* My Bible sits open on my dresser to remind me of the verses I need to memorize; instead, I go right on past, unheeding. The kids think it's hilarious that every Thursday night finds me tooling around in my wheelchair with my Bible on my lap, trying to make up for lost time.

Our latest venture was memorizing Psalm 121, a portion of Scripture that reminds us that God is the only help we can depend on, day and night. During this time I had been stewing about my illness and the constant need for doctor appointments and endless tests. As I waited outside one morning for my ride, I raised my "eyes to the hills" and felt God saying to me, "It's okay. I will help you. I promised you that in Psalm 121."

I used to memorize verses just to be biblically knowledgeable, but now I realize that the real purpose for committing Scripture to memory is so I can be reminded that God really does care about me, whatever I'm going through, right where I am.

Thank You, God, for Your creation and thank You most of all for Your written Word. Amen.

Marcia Van't Land has had articles published in numerous magazines. Formerly an English and physical education teacher, Marcia has written the book *Ya Gotta Have Hope*, which details her progressive neuromuscular disease. She is married and the mother of three children. The Van't Lands reside in Chino, California.

Foot-in-Mouth Disease

Shirley Pope Waite

Set a guard over my mouth, O Lord;
keep watch over the door of my lips.
Psalm 141:3, *NIV*

None of the parents liked that Little League umpire. No fan was more vociferous than Yours Truly when he walked onto the field. He acted as if he'd just been hired for the World Series.

During one poorly officiated game, the umpire's pants ripped down the back seam.

"Serves him right!" I yelled. I joined other "armchair" participants in laughing at his embarrassment.

Waiting for the game to continue, I turned around to talk with other parents. I spied an acquaintance from my bowling league and asked congenially, "On which team does your boy play?"

She gave me an icy look. "My son isn't old enough for Little League." She added, "My husband is the umpire who just tore his trousers."

This isn't the only outbreak of foot-in-mouth disease I've experienced. Fortunately, as with most contagious ailments, inoculations are available. Here are a few:

- Count to ten before you speak.
- "If you can't say something nice, don't say anything

at all." (That's advice from Flower, the little skunk in Walt Disney's *Bambi*.)

- "If you want to stay out of trouble, be careful what you say." (Proverbs 21:23, *TEV*)

Periodically, I ask myself, "Isn't it time for a booster shot?" One good inoculation is Psalm 141:3. I've committed it to memory and find that it protects me from serious outbreaks of this deadly disease.

Thank You, Lord, for the wonderful advice in Your Holy Word. Help me to store it in my mind so that I will live a life pleasing to You. Amen.

Shirley Pope Waite has been published in several books and magazines and teaches at area community colleges. She is a lay minister for her church and enjoys reading and crossword puzzles. Shirley and her husband, Kyle, have six children and make their home in Walla Walla, Washington.

Home, Daddy, Home

Laurie Skye Wardwell

O Lord, I love the habitation of Thy house,
and the place where Thy glory dwells.
Psalm 26:8, *NASB*

My husband and daughter snuggled on the loveseat; this was their special time. They were reading the story of a little boy who wanted to run away from home. He wanted to find some place where he felt needed and loved—where people didn't make him feel bad. My daughter looked pensive, then concerned, as the little boy's friend tried to convince him not to run away.

Lance seized the moment with our daughter to teach her about our Lord. "Morgan, where is a place we can go that we are loved and won't feel bad?"

He was thinking of heaven, but our daughter had a precious lesson and gift for us. She thought for a moment, then with big, serious eyes, she turned, looked up at her father, and said, "Home, Daddy, that's the place, home."

Tears sprang to my eyes; Lance's were misty, too. Home is meant to be a place where we feel loved and accepted. We were touched by Morgan's confidence and assurance in us and in the fact that our daughter felt loved and accepted in our home.

Sometimes, when my life gets hectic, I feel like that little boy. I just want to run away to a place where I will be loved and accepted. Morgan's words reminded me that I don't have to wait to get to heaven to be loved and accepted. For now, I can run into the Lord's presence when life is rough. My heavenly Father is waiting for me. He longs for me to spend time with Him, in prayer and in the study of His Word. When I say, "Home, Daddy, home," He opens His arms and I step into His glorious presence.

Lord, I choose to come to You when I need to be refreshed. I want to dwell with You now and forever. Amen.

Laurie Skye Wardwell is married to Lance and has two young daughters. She enjoys reading, singing, cross-stitch, and spending time with friends and family. She also enjoys speaking to women's groups. The Wardwells make their home in Reedley, California.

Always Room for More

Ellen Weber

*One thing I ask of the Lord, this is what I
seek: that I may dwell in the house of the
Lord all the days of my life, to gaze upon
the beauty of the Lord and to seek him
in his temple.* Psalm 27:4, *NIV*

Although my daughter's tenth-grade
class decided on a big dinner and dance to celebrate the
end of middle school and their promotion into senior
high, Tanya was reluctant to attend. She talked it over
with some Christian friends, and they decided against
putting out the $30 each it would cost for a meal and an
evening of hard-rock music they wouldn't enjoy.

"If my place would hold the girls, I'd have a sleep-
over party," I said to my 75-year-old friend, Pearl, not
anticipating her reply: "Tanya is welcome to have her
friends overnight for a party at my home." Thrilled, Tanya
called her five closest friends and they immediately
planned the menu and chose a Christian film to rent.

On the night of the party, the girls piled in with
sleeping bags, pillows, and enough luggage for the week
and set up camp in the downstairs rumpus room.

"Now don't worry about noise," Pearl said. "My room
is actually soundproof."

The girls ate pizza and sipped diet Cokes on the patio. Then they watched a video, played the piano, and clobbered each other with pillows. Well after midnight they had a Bible study and a summing-up of the school year together.

As I crawled into bed late that night, I thought of all the times Pearl's home had been a shelter to me. I would often call Pearl or pop over and just share coffee or a muffin, while we discussed some book or related an idea to Scripture. Pearl usually spoke of God's unconditional love during those visits, and I would feel love's vivid expression from her life again and again.

Now, with Pearl's welcome mat spread to my daughter and her friends, I thought of how special that home was, with always room enough for more. And I gave thanks for God's house, too, with its welcome mat forever spread out for me.

Lord, thank You for having a home big enough for all of us and thank You for always welcoming Your children. Amen.

Ellen Weber, a former high school teacher, has authored five books and over two-hundred articles. In addition, she writes high school curriculum and is currently completing an M.Ed. in Curriculum Design. Ellen and her daughter Tanya make their home in Victoria, British Columbia.

Accentuate the Positive

Grayce L. Weibley

*But I trust in your unfailing love; my heart
rejoices in your salvation. I will sing to the
Lord, for he has been good to me.*
Psalm 13:5-6, *NIV*

Another writer gave me a copy of a
worksheet she used to give to her students. I read the list
of suggested writing topics and, as I responded to each, I
became dismayed.

The saddest day. How could I select such a day when
sad days had been more numerous than supermarket
products?

The happiest day. Those days fade into oblivion as
crises march across the horizon. Not one outstanding.

Never felt rejected until. I have always felt rejected. It
began when mother pulled my arm from its socket when
I was two. Daddy died when I was three. I went through
two legal adoptions, step-father abuse, and eventually
was kicked out when mother married for the third time.

The loneliest day. Funny thing, I'm lonely in a crowd,
but very comfortable alone with the Bible, a good book,
or my needlecraft.

Parental love. In my estimation, it simply didn't exist.

Anger. As a child, I soon learned that passive

acceptance of life's jolts diminishes anger.

The day I felt closest to God. Now this last item really caught my attention. I reflected on the various times that the Lord had blessed me with an unusual amount of His warming presence. My heart overflowed in gratitude as I tried to focus on one special day.

What about the day that His calm assurance quieted my spiritual and physical heart as I lay in intensive care with a heart attack?

And then there was the time when the surgeon said I wasn't expected to pull through the operation. I felt no fear because I was confident in God's loving care and knew that my life was in His hands.

But tragedies have no monopoly on God's nearness. I remember walking out on the hotel balcony in Spain on a beautiful moonlit night. I reveled in God's magnificent creation. Then, as I looked over the olive grove below, with the mountains beyond, I thought of the Garden of Gethsemane. How much my view resembled that sacred spot. For sometime I stood there praising and thanking God for all that He had done. A holy hush seemed to envelop me.

How blessed I am that in spite of what's happened in my life, I can still rejoice in His salvation and sing praises for His goodness.

Lord, thank You that I can trust in Your unfailing love. My heart, indeed, rejoices in Your salvation, and I will sing to You. Amen.

Grayce L. Weibley is the author of numerous devotions, articles, and stories. She has taught Sunday School for over fifty-five years, is married, and has two children. Grayce enjoys reading and needlecrafts. The Weibleys make their home in Oley, Pennsylvania.

The Wrong Number

Jean Westlake

*Shew me thy ways, O Lord; teach me
thy paths.* Psalm 25:4, *KJV*

I dialed long distance, and, as the telephone was ringing, excitement welled up within me: I was going to talk to my daughter and grandchildren.

A voice answered, "Hello," and I blurted out, "Hi, how are you?" She answered hesitantly, "Pret-ty go-od." "How is everyone?" I asked. She replied, "Fi—ne." "How are the kids?" The response came back, "All right."

Suddenly, I realized I did not recognize the voice on the other end of the line and I enquired, "Whom am I speaking to?" "Becky," she answered softly. I sensed there was a hurt, a need, so I quickly said, "I've dialed the wrong number, but please stay on the line. Don't hang up! Let's talk for a few minutes. Are you all right?"

To allay her fears, I gave her some personal information about myself, and then Becky began to open up. It turned out that she had just graduated from the same Christian college I had attended years ago. Encouraged by this "coincidence," she then confided that her wedding day, planned for summer, had been cancelled and that her mother had recently passed away.

Being the youngest of fifteen children and a long way from home, she was feeling very lonely.

We talked for a long time, and, as the Lord prompted me, I assured her that Jesus was with her. I reminded her that He could take away the loneliness and fill her life with Himself, just as He had promised in Hebrews 13:5: "I will never leave thee, nor forsake thee." I then shared with Becky that God had a plan for her life, and, as she prayed and read the Word of God, the Lord would show her what to do and teach her His Way.

We prayed together for guidance. Then we began praising and thanking God for showing Becky His truth. Her voice became happy and she exclaimed, "You've made my day!"

Oh, to be a blessing to others. I am so glad the "wrong number" was the right number.

Thank You, Lord, for making me a channel of blessing. Help me to be aware of the needs of others. Continue to teach me to be obedient to Your Spirit. Amen.

Jean Westlake is a writer, speaker, musician, and counselor. In addition, she and her husband, George, co-host a television program entitled "Sunday Night Alive" in Kansas City. The Westlakes have four grown children and make their home in Lee's Summit, Missouri.

Retreat

Marcy Weydemuller

Be Thou to me a rock of habitation, to
which I may continually come.
Psalm 71:3, *NASB*

It is early morning and fog blankets
the shore, shading it in varieties of gray. I curl up on a
ledge in the craggy rocks overlooking the beach to watch
the surf.

Rolling waves crash heavily on outer rocks, rushing
in to shore where they slap at the sand. In this quietness,
the rushing sound drowns out all others. Even the water
is gray this morning, dotted with white-foamed waves.

As the waves whirl and splash over exposed tidal
pools, they leave little rivulets of water trickling through.
Just offshore is a small rock topped with lichen which
springs back after each wave tries to push it off. The
lichen bends way over under the force of the waves and
pops back up shaking out arcs of water.

Two seagulls sway and glide silently above the water.
There is a small, drab bird about the size of a robin
patiently searching for food in one of the littlest tidal
pools. The camouflage is so complete that it's difficult to
see it moving. Only slivers of white at the base of its
wings help distinguish it from the rocks.

The mist falls in soft raindrops on my face and hands. Rocks are damp and slick and the dampness is seeping into my clothes, but even though the wind is brisk, I do not want to leave.

The small bird has finished seeking its nourishment, and, as it flies upwards, it bursts with radiant beauty. Under its wings the body is snow white and its brightness gleams.

What is it about this place that always makes me feel renewed? Today is cold, damp, gray, and, yet, it feels invigorating. There's on-going life here despite the outer appearances. The strength and power of the beach remind me of God's power and strength, and that, like the small bird, I too am part of His creation. Here, marbled cliffs remind me of the varieties of people, personalities, opportunities, and choices life offers. In this place of solitude there's a chance to be still, to listen, to reevaluate decisions and goals—a place to retreat in order to return.

Thank You, Lord, that I may always come to You whenever I am empty. You give me Your perspective and Your peace and strengthen me to meet the day's needs. Amen.

Marcy Weydemuller writes book reviews, devotions, and short stories. She is a full-time homemaker and has led various Bible studies. Marcy enjoys reading, crocheting, and cross-stitch. She and her husband, Bob, have three children and reside in Concord, California.

Fruit in Old Age

Louise B. Wyly

They will still bear fruit in old age, they will stay fresh and green. Psalm 92:14, *NIV*

When I was a child, my parents let me plant a plum tree. I looked forward to the time when I could pick juicy, purple plums from that tree. Finally, the tree produced a rich crop of plums, and I ate them in great quantities. But after many fruitful years, that tree grew old and no longer bore fruit. Its fruitful years had ended.

In Psalm 92, the writer paints a picture of a righteous woman, who, unlike my aged, fruitless plum tree, was like a palm tree. Now, palm trees don't bear fruit until fully mature, usually after fifty years of age. Some palm trees don't even start to bear fruit until they are one hundred years old! And we're told that the older the palm tree gets, the sweeter its fruit will be.

The Psalmist goes on to say that the righteous will grow like a cedar of Lebanon planted in the house of the Lord. Cedar trees are strong and live long lives. They weather mountain storms because their roots are continually refreshed by underground springs. They never lose their leaves. Imagine old, gnarled, yet, majestic trees, ever pointing upward toward God!

This encourages me. Since I belong to Christ, I can have the confidence that I will flourish like a palm tree and grow like a cedar of Lebanon planted in the house of the Lord. Trees aren't usually planted in houses, but I will be tenderly watched over in God's house—planted in paradise!

Charles W. Spurgeon wrote: "Every aged Christian is a letter of commendation to the immutable fidelity of Jehovah."

Like the palm tree that bears fruit in old age and the cedar that stays fresh and green, I want to continue to attest to the faithfulness of my God. And as I walk day by day, my fruit will praise Him in all the seasons that remain.

Lord, continue to keep me abiding in You, so that I may continue to bear sweet fruit in old age, and thus bring You the honor and the glory that is due Your name. Amen.

Louise B. Wyly is the writer of over seventy-five articles and devotions for adults and children, and she has authored four books for children. In addition, she enjoys china painting, knitting, crocheting, swimming, and making dolls. She and her husband, Grayson, have four children and reside in Minneapolis, Minnesota.

But, I'm Not Tired!

Paula Yingst

Forgive my hidden faults. Keep your servant also from willful sins; may they not rule over me. Psalm 19:12-13, *NIV*

"I'm not tired!" Katie's heavy-lidded, brown eyes scowled up at her mother, and her usually smiling mouth slouched into a frown. Even though she emphatically denied her fatigue, it was easy to understand why her mood had suddenly turned dour.

From the front passenger seat of our mini-van, I observed the exchange between my dear friend, Paulette, and her seven-year-old daughter. The two of them, along with nine-year-old Scott, had just completed a seven-hour journey from Kansas to California. Taking into account the two-hour time difference and Katie's eagerness to be reunited with her Marine father in Okinawa in a few days, her irritable disposition did not seem unreasonable.

As my husband chauffeured us from the San Diego airport toward our home in Vista (another hour added to Katie's already long day), I assured Paulette that Chuck and I weren't offended by our young guest's cranky behavior. In fact, it was reassuring to know that the "I'm not tired!" attitude is not unique to our own children.

323

The next morning, as I confronted myself in the bathroom mirror, blow dryer in hand, Katie's words kept persistently tugging at my thoughts. A thread of irritation began winding through my emotions and I wondered, *Why is this weighing so heavily on my mind?*

"I'm not tired!" I heard my son Jon insist from the recesses of my memory. Power struggles. Neglected responsibilities. Tears flowing out of confusion and frustration. "I'm not tired!" my daughter Lisa's voice echoed. Late-night studies. Unrealistic expectations. Compassionate weeping for the problems of peers.

But those things are in the past, I lectured my troubled brain. We had lived through them, forgiven each other for them, grown from them. Why was I still feeling their burdening weight?

"I'm not tired!" intruded another memory voice—mine. Shamefully, I realized my own defiance, recalling times when I had boldly uttered those words to my heavenly Father. How many blessings have I forfeited by closing my ears to His wise advice, ignoring His invaluable guidance, allowing myself to become too anxious, too fragmented, too...tired?

Thank You, Father, for loving and leading in spite of my willful attitude. Please help me to trust in Your unfailing wisdom and faithfulness. Amen.

Paula Yingst has written young children's curriculum, devotions, and several articles. She is a creative writing and communication consultant in her school district. Paula and her husband, Chuck, have one daughter and one son and make their home in Vista, California.

Flowers of the Field

Nancy Zegelin

As for man, his days are as grass: as a
flower of the field, so he flourisheth. For the
wind passeth over it, and it is gone, and the
place thereof shall know it no more. But the
mercy of the Lord is from everlasting to
everlasting upon them that fear him, and
his righteousness unto children's children.
Psalm 103:15-17, *KJV*

Too often, our lives seem like the
grass of spring that is green briefly and then quickly turns
brown or like the wildflowers that flourish on the hillside
and wither before anyone notices them.

Sometimes, we encounter daily frustrations that make
our efforts seem entirely worthless. We clean the house
in the morning only to find that by the end of the day it's
dirty again. We teach a Sunday School class only to find
that the children are inattentive and restless and our
efforts seem to be in vain.

We plan an activity or craft only to have it seem a
failure with the group it was intended to teach. Or
sometimes we work on a project and find that our efforts
were hardly needed at all. Yet we never really know

what the eternal effects of our work are. We don't see the whole picture.

When I was a child, I went to the county fair. There, they had a pinball game in which the players were to make the horses race across the board. The first horse to get across was the winner. I pulled the bar that made my horse move. I saw nothing. I pulled it again as quickly as I could. Still nothing. I pulled my bar a few more times and then gave up.

The person in charge asked me why I had stopped. I told her that nothing was happening, as I had expected to see some sort of simulated horse galloping by. In response, she pointed out the horse-shaped lights that were over my head. Each time I had pulled the metal bar, another light had lit up. My horse had not only been near the end of the race, I had almost been a winner.

We are the sowers of God's seeds. Sometimes it's years before our seeds bear fruit. We may not even know, this side of heaven, the true roles we have played in God's kingdom or what fruit He has used our lives to produce. It's good to remember that though we feel our efforts at times are useless and even wonder if our lives count, God has a purpose for our lives. And He sees the whole picture.

Lord, when I'm feeling like I want to give up in the work You've given me to do, remind me that You know the beginning from the end. Your mercy is everlasting. Amen.

Nancy Zegelin has written several short stories and a novel. She enjoys music, sewing, and conducting children's activities. Nancy and her husband have five children and make their home in San Jose, California.

Special Thoughts

Special Thoughts

Special Thoughts

Special Thoughts

Special Thoughts

Special Thoughts

Special Thoughts

Special Thoughts

Special Thoughts

Songs From The Heart is available to your church or organization for fund-raising. Call and inquire about our quantity discounts.

And when you do, ask about *Time Out!*, our popular men's devotional. A collection of writings by 40 men, including several best-selling authors, *Time Out!* is also available at quantity discounts for fund-raising.

Then, watch for *Sing A New Song*, book 2 in the women's series based on the Book of Psalms. *Sing A New Song* is scheduled for release in the spring of 1991.

Are you a writer? Would you like to be considered as a contributor in our next series of devotionals? Write today for guidelines.

Evergreen Communications, Inc.
2085-A Sperry Avenue
Ventura, California 93003
(805) 650-9248

Watch for other 1990 Evergreen releases:

Help for Hurting Moms
by Kathy Collard Miller

What Believers Must Know to Grow
by Tom Carter

Evangelical Jargon
by Tom Carter

Ageless Inspirations
by Ellie Busha